Learning to Live

Copyright © 2016 DB PRESS
All rights reserved.

ISBN: 0-9973115-2-5
ISBN 13: 978-0-9973115-2-5
Library of Congress Control Number: 2016903217
LCCN Imprint Name: DB PRESS, Vancouver, Washington

Learning to Live

20 Lessons from a Therapist on Learning to Live a Better Life

Daniel Bates, LMHC, MAML

Dedicated to my clients,
all of who have taught me about
myself and others.

Table of Contents

Introduction 1

Learning to Communicate 4

Learning to Make Your Marriage Last 10

Learning to Be Compassionate 16

Learning to Ground Yourself in Reality 21

Learning to Respect Your Partner 29

Learning the Art of Connection 35

Learning to Think 41

Learning to Forgive 47

Learning to Set a Goal and Make It Happen 52

Learning the Importance of Feedback 58

Learning About Abusive Relationships and What to Do if You're in One 64

Learning to Recognize the Patterns and Roles that Hurt Your Family 69

Learning to Be Proactive So You Don't Have to Be Reactive 75

Learning the Connection Between Spirituality and Health 82

Learning to Deal with Stress 90

Learning the Power of Vulnerability 96

Learning the Power of Identity 102

Learning to Grieve and Adapt 107

Learning to Control What You Can, Not What You Can't 112

Learning How to Identify What Hurts Your Sex Life . 118

Epilogue 124

About the Author 125

More from Daniel Bates 126

Introduction

Life is many things. It is hard. It is filled with joy. It goes on whether you like it or not. It flies by and proceeds achingly slow. It can seem haphazard and chaotic. Or, innately beautiful and orderly.

Life cannot be controlled by you. It will not bend to your will. But this truth does not make life your enemy. It can be your teacher if you let it.

Most experiences, good or bad, contains within them lessons. These lessons can be hard to perceive and receive. But they contain the wisdom to transform your life. Each chapter in this book walks through a lesson I've discovered while helping clients process and work through the challenges. In the particularity of their struggles, there is help and insight that applies to all.

But lessons don't come easy. Sometimes you must dig *into* the pain to find it. That "digging" is the learning process. It involves understanding, insight, observations, feedback, reflections, and knowledge. This is the learning process. However, it's not all pain. Applying what you've learned from past or present lessons, helps you change. The difficulty is that you may not want to discover certain things about yourself. You may not want to see yourself in an unflattering way. Yet, those who experience change in their lives don't let discomfort get in the way. They've learned uncomfortable truths enable growth.

Learning to Live discusses various self-help topics such as communication, parenting, making goals and being happy. I draw upon my experience working with families, couples and individuals, who have dealt with a range of issues like drug addiction, toxic relationships, poor communication, conflict resolution, parenting issues, and mental health disorders. These lessons aren't an instruction manual, but a navigational tool. They can guide you on your journey to a better life.

Each chapter is roughly five pages. At times, I bring up fascinating studies from the social sciences or my own anecdotal observations from my clinical practice. The name, age and gender of each example client has been changed in order to protect their confidentiality. Stories used in this book are not based on any one person, but are an amalgamation of personal and professional experiences. Furthermore, I try to provide substantive information without getting too academic. The point of this book is to provide you with practical information to get "unstuck."

You can read this book in sequential order, however, this book is not intended to be read that way. Each chapter stands alone. I recommend skimming through the table of contents to find the topic that most relates to what you are interested in or experiencing. Each chapter is like a therapy session in book format. So, if you want to know more about parenting, jump down to the parenting chapter. In that chapter I share with you what I would generally advise parents to do if they came to see me for counseling. If you struggle with motivation and sticking to a goal, skip over to the goal chapter to learn how I help clients set goals and make them happen.

Learning to Communicate

The great thing is to know when to speak and when to keep quiet.

Seneca

What did you say? Huh? I didn't hear you. If you've ever had a spouse, friend or family member accuse you of being a bad listener, this is the chapter for you. If you've ever walked away from a conversation wondering what the other person said, this is the chapter for you. If you've ever walked away from a conversation frustrated that the other person didn't listen to you, this is the chapter for you. In case you missed it, I think this chapter is for you.

Communication has two sides, much like two sides of a coin. The first side is what you say, or verbal communication. The other side is how you communicate with your body, nonverbal communication. Let's jump into the ins and outs of non-verbal communication.

Nonverbal Communication

Nonverbal communication is responsible for 80 percent of communication, although there is some debate as to the exact numbers: some have suggested the 55/38/7 formula,[1] meaning that communication is

---

[1] https://www.psychologytoday.com/blog/beyond-words/201109/is-nonverbal-communication-numbers-game. Retrieval: November 25th, 2015.

composed of 55 percent body language, 38 percent tone of voice and 7 percent actual words spoken. Others have suggested the 60/40 formula,[2] which says that communication is 60 percent facial and 40 percent vocal. Whatever number you accept as true, you have to acknowledge the fact that nonverbal communication[3] (facial expressions, body movement and posture, gestures, eye contact, touch) composes the majority of what communication is.

Nonverbal communication is defined by the messages you send with your body. It plays a key role in how people communicate. It can either damage or undermine what you say. And frankly, it's easy to derail your own communication. Why? We can all be lazy when it comes to communicating. We want to pay lip service to whoever is in front of us and hope that is enough. In other words, we often say the right thing while sending contradictory messages through our nonverbal communication. Therefore, your nonverbal communication will always betray your true intentions.

Let me give you an example of this. I met someone who I really liked. But at the end of our conversations, I walked away feeling glum. I realized that when I spoke with this friend he made very little eye contact. In fact, when he spoke to me, even though he was responding to what I said, he was looking and gesturing to other people. Verbally, he was tracking with me. Saying things like "Yeah… Right… I hear ya." But with his body he was communicating that at best distracted, at worst,

---

[2] Ibid.
[3] http://www.helpguide.org/articles/relationships/nonverbal-communication.htm. Retrieval: December 5th, 2015.

had no interest in what I was saying. Even though he was saying words that showed engagement in the conversation, his eye contact, body posture and position suggested "I couldn't care less." And trust me, I got the message. Our friendship didn't last long.

Verbal Communication

Imagine you are trying to get your troops across a drawbridge into an enemy's castle. And right as you're about to storm across, the castle's defenses are raised and the drawbridge is pulled up. Your troops go *kersplatt* into the moat! Doesn't communication feel like this sometimes?

Let's say you have an issue with your spouse, friend, family member or co-worker. You really want the other person to understand what's bugging you. You give them the message, but instead of getting through to them, your message hits a wall. They get defensive and your message gets forgotten in the fight. So frustrating, right? Is there a better way?

Thankfully, there is. Instead of getting mad at the other person for not receiving your message, ask yourself why it was hard for them to listen in the first place. Often, we can lace our message with hidden judgments or accusations without even realizing it. It could be tone of voice, the way the message is framed or a subtle attack. Either way, the result is the same: the receiver gets defensive. Here's a method for circumventing defenses—I call it the *Sandwich Method*.

Imagine if you will the basic components of a sandwich. You've got your bun on top, some kind of meat in the middle, with another bun on the bottom.

Just like a sandwich, there are three components to effective communication. Let's examine the first part of this communication sandwich:

Step 1: The first part in the *Sandwhich Method* of communication is the top bun. Start off your conversation by saying something positive about what the other person has been doing:

"Thank you so much for your work around the house lately."

"I've noticed you've been eating healthier over the past few weeks."

Or share a way in which you understand or can relate to the receiver: "I know work has been totally crazy for you this week."

"I understand you haven't slept well the last few nights."

Starting off with the first bun cushions your feedback. It buffers the other person's defenses, helping them to listen to what you have to say. It also puts you in a frame of mind that is more positive than punitive, which will come across nonverbally as well. Win-win!

Ask yourself: *Are you so eager to get to your point that you neglect the positives the other person has done?*

Step 2: This is the meat or middle portion of the sandwich. At this point you deliver the feedback or request that, said without the first bun, would raise the other person's defenses. However, when using the *Sandwich Method* you will instead sidestep defenses by saying an *"I" Statement*. An *"I" Statement* is a way of giving feedback by explaining your feelings as a result of the situation or the other person's behavior. The basic structure of the *"I" Statement* is "I feel [name an emotion] because [explain the situation]." This differs from a *"You" Statement*, which is more of an attack filled with accusations, absolute statements or complaints.

"I feel frustrated and lonely when you come home and focus all your attention on social media."

Or you can use the "I" Statement in reverse: "When you ask me so many questions right when I get home from work, I feel overwhelmed and cornered."

Using *"I" Statements* allows the other person to understand what specific behaviors are the problem, and what is your experience of the behaviors. Also, you are being specific while not giving any labels or judgments, just factual descriptions of the other person's behaviors and your response to them.

Ask yourself: *Do you give the other person judgments or descriptions when giving them feedback?*

Step 3: This is the bottom bun of the sandwich. This is the point at which you make a direct request of the other person, help them think of alternatives to the offensive behavior and share how you will support them. This may entail some negotiation:

"If you could focus on me and not on social media when you get home, it would mean a lot to me. And I'll be better about not getting sucked into Facebook or Twitter, too."

"If you could give me some time to decompress when I get home after a long day, I'll be more willing and open to connect with you."

A complete sandwich method statement looks something like this: "I know work has been crazy for you lately and you rarely have any free time. Yet, when you come home and get on Facebook for hours, it really frustrates me. I miss you and want to connect. If you could come home and spend some time with me, I won't be on your case when you log on to Facebook, and I'll be better about not spending too much time on social media, too."

This is just one example. Your statement could look very different. Personally, I have seen the benefits of using the *Sandwich Method* first-hand in the way I communicate. Professionally, the *Sandwich Method* is my go-to solution when I'm working with a family or couple that struggles with communication.

Ask yourself: *Do you only focus on what the other person needs to do, forgetting your part in the problem and what you need to change?*

The *Sandwich Method* makes difficult conversations doable. I don't say "easy," because difficult conversations are always difficult, but using the *Sandwich Method* will help. And don't be afraid to modify the method in whatever way works for you. Even though I'm giving you a formula, don't use it like one. Use it like a roadmap. There are many routes to reach the same destination: so match your nonverbal communication with your message and give the *Sandwich Method* a try. Don't let communication become warfare.

Learning to Make Your Marriage Last

*A journey is like marriage.
The certain way to be wrong is to think you control it.*
John Steinbeck[4]

Let's face it. Your chances of staying married aren't good. Sorry for sounding bleak. But first-time marriages have a 41 percent[5] chance of ending in divorce—and it only gets worse after that. For second-time marriages, the rate of failure rises to 60 percent, and third-time marriages dissolve 73 percent of the time. There is one divorce every 36 seconds; 100 divorces every hour; 2,400 divorces per day; 16,800 divorces per week; 876,000 divorces per year. I told you this was going to sound bleak.

So, here's the good news. The fate of some does not have to be your fate. Yet avoiding the path to divorce isn't easy. Marriage is hard work and it requires change. Many people aren't prepared for this. They expect marriage always to be fun, easy and enjoyable. That simply isn't the truth. So, here are few ideas to help make your marriage last:

Being Right Isn't Always the Answer

---

[4] Demakis, Joseph (2014). *The Ultimate Book of Quotations*, p. 310. Kindle Edition.
[5] http://www.mckinleyirvin.com/Family-Law-Blog/2012/October/32-Shocking-Divorce-Statistics.aspx. Retrieval: December 12th, 2015.

I can argue my point 'til I'm blue in the face, but if I'm mean and cruel, what have I really won? If winning an argument comes at the cost of demoralizing your spouse, is it worth it? By winning the battle, you may inadvertently lose the war.

Listen to Understand—Not to Build Counter-arguments

I've recently started the habit of asking myself this very important question: "Am I listening to my wife in order to understand her, or am I just building ammunition for my own argument?" Ask yourself this question and come back to reality. Nothing ever gets resolved if neither party is listening in a meaningful attempt to understand the other person's perspective.

Choose Your Battles!

This one sounds tired and overused but—oh, man—will it save your bacon! Simply put, some battles don't need to be fought. When you're not sure what to do, ask yourself two questions: "Am I more invested in the object of this battle than my spouse is? And if I'm not, can I simply just trust my spouse with this issue?" Learn to trust your spouse's judgment. Some battles aren't worth fighting. Learn to let go of control.

Make Apologies—Without Qualifications

I learned this one the hard way. In the past, when apologizing to my wife for my mistakes, I would often couch my apologies in all the reasons *why* I did what I did. Don't apologize while simultaneously justifying your actions. This is not a true, authentic apology. When apologizing, remove the word "but" from your vocabulary.

Take Ownership for Your Actions

This may come as a surprise, but you are not perfect! You have no one to blame for your actions but yourself. *You control you.* Regardless of how your spouse acts, you are ultimately responsible for how you behave. Stop blaming your spouse for your actions and reactions. Take ownership.

Replace Judgments with Feedback about Behavior

When giving feedback to your spouse, some of the worst things you can say are "You, liar!" or "You're irrational" or "You're so selfish." We all want to say these things, but it never ends well when we do. Why? Because these are *labels*, judgments on a person's character. They are meant to damage, not to clarify or help. Instead, give your spouse feedback on his or her behavior and how that behavior affected you.

Be Flexible!

If you didn't want to change, you shouldn't have gotten married! Marriage is the laboratory of life. It is the place where you try new things, make mistakes and learn valuable lessons. You cannot *not* be changed by it. So, let marriage do its work. If you won't change for your spouse, who would you change for? Who better to change for than your spouse?

Assume the Best

I've made the mistake of holding on to my wife's past mistakes. Each time a new issue arises, all past mistakes come flooding to my mind, giving an added intensity to every fight. I jump to conclusions, thinking she has "messed up again." Such behavior simply isn't fair and it predisposes a couple to look only for the negative. Assuming the best of your spouse sets you up for success and helps you see all the positives.

Becoming the Right Person, Not *Being* the Right Person

I think the growth process in marriage isn't about *being* the right person, but *becoming* the right person for your spouse—within reason, of course. If your spouse is asking you to become a drug dealer, terrorist or contract killer, then yes, my idea breaks down. Yet, if your spouse is asking you to be more consistent, become a better listener, follow a budget, back them up on parenting choices, pick up after yourself, and stop pet-peeve behaviors, then change for them. Even though you may disagree, if the person is of value to you, then you should value what is important to them.

While this idea accords with common sense, in no way do I think it is an easy thing to do. You wouldn't believe how many couples I've counseled who have struggled with it. The reason is that valuing what the other person values might require change. Valuing what your partner values doesn't mean you have to give up your values. It doesn't mean you have to become another person. Yet, it is important to understand that there is a set of values that each person brings to every relationship. And some of those individual values may have to take second place to the values of the relationship.

I once worked with a couple who sought counseling to restore trust. Each partner had broken trust by having a sexual relationship with someone outside the marriage. As you can imagine, trying to rebuild trust after an affair can be very difficult. We had to examine why the affairs happened. I pointed out to the couple that the affairs happened, in part, because each of them prioritized their own values and needs above the values and needs of the relationship. They allowed the relationship to wither by not tending to it properly. Thus, the relationship was unsatisfying— they're needs weren't being met. So, they satisfied those needs with other people. And with that came serious consequences.

When they came to me, they needed to rebuild their relationship from the ground up. They both needed to start sacrificing their individual priorities for the priorities of the relationship to make it work. This was hard work to do. It required them rethinking and reevaluating what they valued and wanted. But, with time, they slowly reprioritized the values and needs of the relationship. And with that came long-term success. Rebuilding their relationship was a marathon not a sprint.

But what do I mean by individual values as opposed to relationship values?

Individual values are those goals, needs and desires that apply to just you—where you want to live, work, what you want to eat, how often you want to have sex, how to spend money. For example, you may want to buy a new car every year, and that personally benefits you, but it may not benefit your family or relationship. *If you only consider what benefits you and not what benefits the relationship, you are setting yourself up for disaster.*

There is a tradeoff when it comes to individual and relational values. Sacrificing an individual need for the relationship may hurt in the moment, no one likes being deprived, but the relationship is benefitted and nurtured. And when relationships are properly nourished, individuals are satisfied.

Learning to Be Compassionate

> Be kind, for everyone you meet is fighting a harder battle.
>
> Plato

This chapter is a bit different from the rest in that I discuss my own personal journey with compassion from the perspective of a professional counselor. However, I think this will still be instructive, practical and helpful to you. In the particulars of my story are lessons that apply generally.

When I first started practicing counseling I had a deep sense of empathy for my clients. I understood their struggles and what they were experiencing. I truly cared for them. And even though I lacked confidence, skill and experience, I made up for my professional weaknesses with genuine care for my clients.

Although, my experience is not all that uncommon. Research from the field of social science has demonstrated that younger therapists can actually be more effective than their seasoned counterparts. The reason for the difference is that younger therapists tend to care more genuinely for the person in front of them. Coupling that with the well-established fact that the most important part of counseling is the relationship, you can see why a therapist who genuinely cares and understands their client may actually be more effective than those who are more skilled. Isn't it weird how that works out?

But it's not all roses and daisies from there on out. The longer a therapist practices, the harder and harder it gets to, well, care. Typically, therapists entering the field are working with some of the most challenging populations. To make matters worse, the pay is not very good. At the end of the day, a therapist can feel like they've put out a lot of effort with little to show for it. With the long hours, resistant clients and lack of appreciation, you've got yourself a recipe for burn-out.

But the underlying soul of this experience belongs not solely to mental health counselors. In fact, if you flip through your mental rolodex of relationships, you can probably think of a list of relationships like the one described above: a best friend who made the relationship all about themselves, a spouse who never appreciated you, or a parent who constantly denied a serious problem. If you care at all for these people and want to be helpful to them, you and a counselor have more in common than you may have realized. Likewise, the lessons counselors have learned can work for you.

Compassion Fatigue

It's ironic how the very thing that gets therapists into their field—the desire to help others—ultimately may force them out. The reason counselors leave the field is that it's really hard to help people change, especially those who don't want to change. When you try long enough, care hard enough and hope deep enough and find little results, you may run the risk of *compassion fatigue*. This is not just a therapist thing: it's an everybody thing. Compassion fatigue is the depletion of anyone's psychological, physical and spiritual resources due to caring for others in pain and distress.

The care and empathy I felt so strongly for my clients at the beginning of my career eventually started to wane. I began to grow bitter. I was repulsed by the nasty acts of clients towards their loved ones. I couldn't understand how a person could act so cruelly to their child, spouse or parent. Combine that with low pay, little appreciation, poor outcomes with clients, and self-doubt, I soon hit an empathy wall. I questioned my ability to help another person. I didn't feel confident that I could help someone effect change in their life. I felt powerless. This affected how I practiced. I noticed I was less effective with clients. I would drive home after sessions and just yell. Quickly, I was faced with the question, "How do I keep going?"

This question forced me to look critically at the way I viewed clients and, really, how I viewed people. I realized I was easily ensnared by a negative way of looking at others. The negative perspective creates an impenetrable box. Once I put you in the box, it was hard for me to see you any other way. I have come to see the limitations of the negative perspective in light of a better way of perceiving others: that is, the art of *reframing*.

Reframing

When I learned *reframing*, my life changed. The skill is essentially looking at someone's *worst* behavior for the purpose of finding a *noble intent*, an alternative explanation for bad behavior that is benign or even positive. For example, around the time of his parents' divorce, a teenager uses pot, steals and vandalizes property. Because the parents are so concerned for their child, they put aside their contention and focus on how they can best support their teenager. They decide to co-parent, support each other in front of the teen, and settle the divorce quickly instead of dragging it out. Now, an observer could survey the situation and conclude that the teen is a bad egg, and that his criminal behavior is only added stress to his parents. Or the observer could reframe the child, making the case that the teenager's acting out, in a way, provided a focus that unified the family towards a common goal. The teen's behavior repaired the growing rift in the family. And even though things aren't perfect, they are on a better course than before.

This is a radical way of thinking and not many are comfortable with it. It's easy to get caught in the trap of seeing only the negative. But once I really gave myself to reframing, the skill gave me a way of understanding my clients in the midst of what on the surface appeared to be deplorable behavior. And not only that, it gave me a way of relating to them. I could relate with their struggles. I could see my own struggles in them. Slowly, I sloughed off all the negative ascriptions to their bad behavior and began looking for alternative explanations. And believe it or not, a growing sense of compassion returned. But it wasn't like the care I had at first for my clients. This was a much more resilient and tenacious kind of compassion. The term I've used to describe it is *learned compassion*.

What I mean by *learned compassion* is that before, when I first started, I was relying on a kind of natural compassion. In other words, the situation or plight of the client evoked a feeling of care for them. I didn't have to work at it much. The compassion I felt was something that happened to me. And, as a result, the feeling of compassion quickly faded. What I realized that compassion is not feeling. It is not something that comes to me. It is not caught. It is, however, taught. In that, you can learn, sharpen, mold yourself into a compassionate person. True compassion is developed, as in a skill. It doesn't depend on the client or their situation evoking a feeling of care for them. I can give compassion to a client regardless of who they are, whether they deserve it or not.

But not many think of compassion in this way. Why? We often conceive of compassion in the first way I described it. We act compassionately dependent upon the worthiness of the person. But this, I would argue, is a deficient form of compassion. It's weak and won't get you very far. In order for a therapist to survive in the field, they need to be able to give compassion, as I said before, regardless of the person or situation, or the worthiness of either one. This is a stronger, more profound, more transformative way of practicing compassion for you and for those you encounter.

Genuine and authentic compassion is undergirded by mercy, which is to give someone something they don't deserve. There are people in your life who do not deserve your compassion. To be blunt, giving them compassion hurts. Yet, learned compassion will transform you and those around it, even those who resist, who don't thank you for it, who are underserving.

Therapist or not, we all struggle with being compassionate to those around us, be it a co-worker, child, spouse, friend or relative. We all struggle with only seeing the negative. But do not let that kill your empathy and compassion towards others. I say this from personal experience. When you have numbed yourself from caring about others, you have given up something precious and life-giving. Turning away from others kills your joy. Do not let this happen to you. I implore you to practice reframing. Practice learned compassion. If not for their sake, do it for yourself.

I challenge you to be a person of tenacious, resilient and fearless compassion. Give it regardless of the worthiness of the person in front of you. For, I'm sure, there have been times when you have not been worthy of compassion yourself, but we all need and want it. In the act of giving compassion you will receive more than you give. Compassion frees the burdened soul, of those who give it and who receive it.

Learning to Ground Yourself in Reality

> Grounding and centering are lifelines to reality when the connection to it seemingly slips away.
> Unknown Author[6]

Imagine feeling like everyone you know, everything around you, everything you are thinking and feeling is fake. That what you are experiencing can't be trusted. And instead being in the here-and-now, you feel like a detached observer, watching yourself from a disconnected vantage point and there's no way for you to reconnect yourself and reality. No, this isn't the plot of Christopher Nolan's movie *Inception*. This is a real phenomenon that people deal with every day. And before you start thinking the experience sounds kind of cool, I can assure you, it's not.

Feeling disconnected from reality is an awful experience. When you don't feel connected to your body or thoughts it can feel like you're not in control of yourself, like your detached from reality. In other words, you feel like you can't trust yourself and your surroundings, as if you are losing yourself. Clinical terms used to describe this experience are:

---

[6] The author of this quote is unknown.

- Depersonalization- An internal feeling of disconnection from oneself, i.e. self-estrangement.
- Derealization- An external feeling of disconnection from one's surroundings,
- Dissociation- Detachment from physical and emotional experience.

Depersonalization, derealization and dissociation (what I'll call going forward "DDD") have been informally described as a psychotic break, feeling numb, an out of body experience, or disconnection from reality. The experience of DDD can be short term, lasting a few minutes, or, it can be long-term, lasting years. The experience can be so disorienting that some have committed suicide. Typically, DDD is associated with psychoses, however, people suffering from severe depression, PTSD, Bipolar disorder, drug intoxication, and some personality disorders can cause DDD.

There is a caveat worthy of mention regarding DDD. In a way, DDD can have a survival function. What do I mean by that? When people are experiencing intense trauma, i.e. domestic violence and abuse, rape, warfare, a violent attack and so on, the brain will detach from first-person experience and shift one's perception to that of an observer. And, in some regards, this is a preferable perceptual vantage point than the first-person experience. Think of it, would you want to experience every moment, every pain, every rush of fear, terror, shock and horror of being raped? No, of course not. You'd much rather be detached from the experience. The true horror is when someone doesn't detach, and they experience every excruciating moment of their trauma.

That being said, the experience of DDD in non-trauma situations, that which is persistent and chronic, can make life near impossible. What was once adaptive in a survival situation, becomes maladaptive in normal life. Normal life is filled with emotional experiences, good and bad, that are appropriate to feel. But DDD sabotages normal emotional experience, so that, when you are experiencing joy, pleasure, contentment, happiness, closeness and excitement, the feelings are quickly anesthetized, and replaced with a numb feeling. DDD is an emotional killer. Emotions are critical for healthy functioning. In other words, without emotion you cannot process grief, learn from experience and feel the joys of life.

Also, those suffering from DDD experience intense anxiety because they don't know when an episode of DDD will hit them. And, in fact, the anxiety of not wanting to experience DDD can actually trigger an experience of DDD. This is a vicious cycle that overwhelms and ensnares the DDD sufferer.

So, what can you do if you suffer from DDD? Is there hope? Are there solutions, techniques, and approaches that can help? In short, yes, there is hope. There are things you can do, behaviorally, to help yourself. And, there are professionals that can provide you with counseling and medication that effectively treat DDD.

First things first, I'd first recommend seeing a psychologist to get a mental health evaluation. Based on their assessment, you can see a psychiatrist to get evaluated and prescribed medication that can help. In terms of behavioral interventions that can help you feel grounded and centered, here are my suggestions:

Self-Observation: Now, this may seem like an ironic suggestion since part of the problem is feeling like your an observer. But the point of this is to make first-person observations. Those first-person observations are very grounding. They relocate you in the here-and-now. Self-observations also have to do with recognition. If you can recognize that you are having a DDD episode, you can then intervene on yourself to change your experience. But, this is not possible unless you have awareness of what's happening.

Stay Calm: Once you've recognized you are having a DDD episode, don't panic. Panic is like cement for DDD. If you can remain calm after becoming aware of the DDD episode, you are more likely to work your way out of it.

Radical Acceptance: When you try fighting against DDD, you are actually giving it energy. DDD feeds off of your resistance. Instead, accept that you are having a DDD moment. It's okay to feel numb, or detached. It's not the end of the world. You can work your way out of it.

Positive Self-Talk: After accepting the fact that you are having a DDD moment, talk to yourself in a positive manner. Think of it like this, what would you tell your best friend if they were having a DDD moment? You'd probably say something like "Its going to be okay," "You are safe," "This isn't going to last for forever,"

"Stay calm," "This will be over soon," and "There's hope." Use those same positive messages, but with yourself. In fact, I'd recommend making these positive self-talk statements to yourself throughout the day so that you are prepared for a DDD episode.

Self-Soothing: This concept comes from child developmental psychology. The idea is rather simple, when you are feeling emotionally flooded, regulate your feelings by soothing yourself. So, for example, when a baby is crying and finds their thumb, that is self-soothing. Obviously, I'm not suggesting you start sucking your thumb, but, I do suggest you develop some self-soothing strategies such as deep breathing, physical exercise, watching a favorite TV-show, eating chocolate, talking to a friend and so on. The self-soothing plan can be as unique and particular to you as you want it. If something works, then do it, just as long as you are not harming yourself or another person.

Hopefully, this information is helpful. Please do yourself a favor and do not ignore DDD. It is a mental illness that steals joy and can lead to suicide. However, it is not permanent. There are effective treatments for DDD. Seeing a counselor, working with a psychiatrist, taking medication and using the tips provided above can help. With effort, over time, you will see change.

Learning to Respect Your Partner

> This is the first test of a gentleman: his respect for those who can be of no possible value to him.
>
> William Lyon Phelps[7]

Sometimes partners can get so fed up with each other that they start viewing each other as juvenile. I've heard many wives complain they're raising three kids, two children and a husband. I've had husbands complain to me about their wives, how their always nagging and belittling them. This is not a problem unique to male-female marriages. I've heard the same complaints from all sorts of couples: dating, premarital, long-term married, and remarried. Across the board, partners struggle to give each other respect.

But the more important question remains: *Why* do people act disrespectfully towards those they love the most? Okay, let's stop making this about hypothetical people and be honest with each other. You've been disrespectful to your partner, to your child, to your co-worker, friend or family member at some point in your life. Maybe not all the time, but it's happened and you've regretted it. There could be a million reasons why you do it. But no reason, however justified, can shake that guilty feeling as you walk away after being disrespectful to someone. I'll repeat: whatever the reason, don't treat someone you value disrespectfully.

---

[7] Lyons Press (2014). *1001 Smartest Things Ever Said*, p. 24. Kindle Edition.

Doing so only spells trouble because disrespect breeds disrespect. If someone feels disrespected, hurt and attacked, they will either be defensive or lash back. So, what's the antidote to the poison of disrespect? Look for and affirm the positive when you see it, regardless of how you feel. Effective parents are a good example of this.

Effective parents make a habit of looking for the positive in their kid's behavior, attitude and performance even if their child just acted out. In fact, it is especially important to affirm the positive after a hard moment because it gets you back on track. Affirming the positive encourages the good, while discouraging the bad. When you make a habit of noticing the positive, the more positives you notice. And the more you notice, the more positive stuff happens. Crazy how that works, right?

The same principle effective parents use by increasing their attention to the positive can be used by spouses, partners, dating couples or engaged couples. It's the same idea in a different context.

Spouses and partners: please, do yourself a favor and borrow this strategy and apply it to your relationship. Ask yourself, "Do I only see the negatives in my wife, husband, boyfriend or girlfriend? Why do I do that? What garners the majority of my attention? What patterns am I perpetuating in terms of what I respond to?"

As said in the parent chapter, I am not suggesting that you never respond to the negative. It's healthy to air your grievances, to have conflict and to address problems. Confrontation comforts no one; but often, what doesn't *feel* positive heals and mends. Sometimes the bitter pill is the best medicine. But if you look at your relationships and see only problems, the real problem might be you. The real problem might be the lens through which you look at your partner.

Here are a few ways the negative lens hurts your relationship:
- Only seeing the negative puts your partner in a box that is hard to break free from.
- Only seeing the negative predisposes you to only see more of the negative.
- Only seeing the negative unfairly rules out the positive things your partner does.
- Only seeing the negative blinds you from seeing your own mistakes.

I recommend asking yourself if any of the above is true of you. Sit down with your partner and ask for feedback. What do they think? Would they agree with the above statements regarding you? If one or more bullet points are true of you, take a page out of the effective parent playbook and rebalance what you pay attention to and what you respond to. *Don't ignore the negative, but foster a bias towards the positive.* This might just save your relationship.

Preference versus Right and Wrong

The second and indispensable perspective necessary for couples to respect each other is adopting a "preferences" mindset versus a "right or wrong" mindset. So, what do I mean by that? A "preferences" mindset recognizes there are many things shared between a couple that are not matters of objective truth. Take, for example, preferences regarding birthdays. One person likes having as many people as possible at their birthday party. The other may like a smaller, quieter event. So, is one person right for liking a lot of people at their party, and the other person wrong for wanting only a few people there? Of course not! But time and time again, many couples treat something like birthdays as if there's simply one right way.

I also see many couples make this mistake when they go about making choices regarding scheduling. Again, one person likes to be structured in terms of picking a time and day to do something, and the other likes to be more spontaneous. I ask again: is one right for wanting structure, and the other wrong for wanting spontaneity? Both are expressions of personal values or preferences, and neither reflects the absolute right or wrong way of doing something.

Is a British citizen wrong for wanting to drive on the left side of road? No, of course not—just don't do it in the United States! There are many things that inform our decision-making, like custom, family of origin, culture and personal preference. It's not a matter of right and wrong that British citizens drive on the left side of the road and US citizens drive on the right side of the road. It would be silly to think of one driving custom as right and the other wrong. Yet we use this silly kind of thinking all the time when it comes to differences in our relationships.

That isn't to say there are no "right and wrong" issues in life. Molesting children, embezzling from your company, cheating on your taxes, spreading lies about a competitor: these aren't expressions of personal preferences, but are morally wrong actions. A husband protecting his wife, a child standing up against a bully, a friend keeping you accountable, listening to someone after a loss: these are morally good actions.

But problems start when a partner takes the preference of their partner and puts it in the "wrong" category and places their own preference in the "right" category. This creates conflict and relational damage.

So, what's the solution to the problem? Recognize the difference between "right and wrong" and "preference" issues. For some couples, this is a very hard thing to do. Preferences are things we've learned from our family, culture and community. They are a function of our personality. They are long-held and usually go unchallenged until you get in an intimate relationship.

Recognize the strength amidst the differences in your relationship. There are benefits to your partner's way of doing things. The spontaneous partner has a way of doing things that quickly responds to needs, can be more fun, and is sensitive to the urgency of a situation. The structured partner's approach allows for greater consistency, predictability and longevity.

Each style needs the other in order to compensate for its deficits. Speaking personally, I need my wife because she complements my weaknesses. She is a planner—I most assuredly am not. Time and time again, I am grateful that she possesses a preference and skill for planning that I do not have. And trust me, when you make a major decision in your life, you want a plan. However, at the beginning of our marriage, I was incredibly frustrated with her because I thought she was a kill-joy. She always wanted me to have a plan. She was cramping my style. But eventually, I realized she was actually forcing me to grow. I realized she was the best thing for me. It was then I learned that differences among couples should be cause for appreciation rather than judgment. She added to my life by virtue of being different from me—and I, her. But I was actively limiting the benefit she brought to my life by reacting against her preference for planning. Don't make the same mistake!

Learning the Art of Connection

> Love is not something we give or get; it is something that we nurture and grow, a connection that can only be cultivated between two people when it exists within each one of them—we can only love others as much as we love ourselves.
>
> Brene Brown[8]

Connecting with other people can be tricky. It can feel like a risk because you don't know how the other person will respond. They could embrace you or reject you. Therefore, connection is more of an art than a science. Psychologists have even likened it to a dance. You take a step forward, the other person responds in kind. These "steps" are understood by social psychologists and researchers as "bids." This language has been borrowed from the world of auctioning. It's a fitting metaphor. In a relationship, someone makes an offer or a bid for emotional and relational connection. That bid may be accepted or not.

One man, John Gottman, has tried to bring science to the art form. Gottman is a noteworthy psychologist and relationship researcher at the University of Washington. He has found that when bids for connection are rejected, it makes the possibility of future bids less likely to occur. Put another way, if

---

[8] Brown, Brene (2010). *The Gifts of Imperfection: Let Go of Who You Think You're Supposed to Be and Embrace Who You Are,* Hazelden Publishing, p. 26.

you've just been rejected, you're scared to try again. Manipulation can also decrease or completely neutralize bids for connection. There should be no hidden agenda, exploitation or selfish intent when it comes to love. Yet, people often distort love in this way.

Imagine, for example, if a parent locked their child in the basement with no food until they behaved correctly. Clearly this is wrong and punishable by law. But what is the difference between physical starvation and emotional starvation? I would argue that in some cases, emotional starvation can be just as devastating to the wellbeing and normal development of a child.

This is the premise for the Stephen King novel *Carrie*. Carrie's mother, a religious-fanatic, locked her daughter away with no food for her sinful behavior. After a lifetime of torture from her mom and mockery from her classmates, Carrie finally gets a lucky break. The most popular guy at school asks her to the prom. Well, as the story goes, Carrie and her date win prom King and Queen. Carrie couldn't be happier. She finally feels like she fits in, which makes the truth all the more bitter: while on stage, Carrie is doused with cow's blood and suddenly realizes that the past few months have all been a horrible joke. As she looks around at her jeering classmates, something snaps within her. Carrie unleashes a maelstrom of telekinetic destruction on her school and town, leading to the death of her mother.

Sadly, the story of Carrie is all too real (minus the telekinetic powers). You may not be physically starving your child, spouse, friend or family member, but are you starving them emotionally? Or are you starved and don't know it? Relationship conditioned on good behavior tends to make the bad times very bad. And emotional starvation isn't limited to children—its damaging for adults, too. Everyone, regardless of age, gender, race or income level, needs to belong, needs to be loved and to have connection with others.

Gottman thinks one of the basic human needs is relational connection between people. It's as important as shelter, food and safety. Connection is not a luxury. It's a necessity. And because it's so important, when bids for connection don't work out, the effects are serious. People can turn to addiction, develop serious mental health disorders, or even worse, commit suicide. Therefore, how we respond to the bids of others is very important. But our responses are a little more complicated than acceptance or rejection. According to Gottman, there are three different types of responses to bids.

Three Responses to Bids

The first is *turning towards* someone when they make a bid. This is obviously the most positive response. For example:

- When a wife gets home from work, her husband asks her how her day was. This is a bid for connection. The wife sits down and shares that she had a really stressful day. They talk for a little while longer, and the husband offers to make dinner that night. The wife smiles and gives her husband a big hug.
- When a teenage son does the chores his dad asked him to do plus an extra chore, this is a bid

for connection. Dad sees the extra chore completed and gives his son a high five. Later that day, Dad takes his son out to shoot hoops.

In both examples, something happens that certainly doesn't happen in the next two types of responses to bids. What is it? It is the principle of *reciprocity*. Psychologists have found that when you make a pro-social gesture to someone—such as getting the door, smiling and saying hello, going out of your way to be helpful—people tend to respond in similar ways. You get in return what you put out. It's kind of a like a relational version of karma: what goes around, comes around. If you put out kindness, you're likely to get kindness in return. If you put out respect, you're more likely to get respect in return.

The second type of response is *turning against*. This is the situation in which someone makes a bid for connection and the other person responds with hostility. Let's look at this response through the two examples mentioned earlier.

- Wife comes home; husband asks how her day was. She explodes on him for not giving her space.
- Teenage son does his chores and one extra. Dad sees the chores but scolds his son for doing them improperly.

This kind of response does serious relational damage. Gottman has found that relationships characterized by this response style end quickly. Why is this? Making a bid for connection is a vulnerable thing to do. The bidder is allowing themselves to be wounded in order to connect with the other person. So, the other person's response matters. Think of it like a knight taking off his armor. An attack when the knight's armor is off does far more damage than when it is on.

The third type of response is *turning away*. Here, when someone makes a bid for connection, the other person's response is distance. Let's look at this response through the two examples mentioned earlier.

- Husband asks his wife how her day was. She doesn't look at him. She walks upstairs to her bedroom and lies down. Husband follows her up and again asks how she is doing. She turns the TV on and ignores him.
- Teenage son does more than asked. Dad sees the chores and makes no comment. He doesn't praise or thank his son.

This kind of response can also be a relationship-killer. *Turning against* ends relationships in fireworks; *turning away* ends relationships through a slow burn.

Ask yourself: are you emotionally and relationally starved? Well, why is that? Have you stopped putting out bids for connection because it's too risky? Are you blind to the bids that others are putting out towards you? Are you now the one turning against or away from the bids of others?

I'm the father of the two daughters, which means I spend a lot of time watching kid shows with my girls. An episode of my oldest daughter's favorite TV show featured a character who was feeling bored and lonely. He went to see his friends, but they were busy with something and didn't want to include him. He became very jealous and followed them around all day. He was so preoccupied with being shut out, he was oblivious to bid of another friend who kept inviting him to play with her.

He discovered that his friends were excluding him because they were getting him a surprise for his birthday. He also realized he had done to his friend what he thought was being done to him: turning away when receiving a bid for connection. This is a corny example from a kid's TV show, but there is a powerful lesson being taught.

Make sure you don't get hyper-focused on your own way of connecting. When I was a teenager, my dad and I had a hard time communicating. I was always annoyed that he didn't show an interest in my passion, visual art. Instead, he would invite me to work with him out in his shop on a woodworking project. After a long period without connection, I decided to join him one evening as he worked on a cabinet. This one-time event became a weekly occurrence. And, as we worked, we also talked. Talking led to vulnerable sharing, and our connection grew stronger. He then offered to build frames for my paintings. We were talking, working with each other on projects of our different passions, and most importantly, forming a positive connection. However, this was only possible because I turned *towards* my dad's bid, even though it wasn't the bid I wanted. Responding towards the bid created a bridge between the two of us. He reciprocated by turning towards my bid for connection through visual arts. So, ask yourself, how do you respond to bids for connection? And are there bids for connection under your nose that you haven't even considered?

Learning to Think

The way we see things is the source of the way we think and the way we act.

Stephen Covey[9]

Your thinking, even when you don't think you're thinking, is hugely important to your mental health. A proverb from Frank Outlaw, the creator of BI-LO, articulated the formative power of one's thoughts well:

Plant a thought and reap a word;
plant a word and reap an action;
plant an action and reap a habit;
plant a habit and reap a character;
plant a character and reap a destiny.[10]

What you *think* trickles down to every aspect of your being. There is no one from human history who preached and modeled this idea more than Socrates. Plato, the Athenian philosopher and a student of Socrates, recorded his teacher's saying "The unexamined life is not worth living." If you accept that the way you think is important, then evaluating *how* you think ought to be high on your priority list, shouldn't it?

---

[9] Covey, Stephen R. (2013). *The 7 of Highly Effective People: Powerful Lessons in Personal Change* (25th Anniversary Edition). Kindle Location 813.
[10] 1885 November 22, The Sunday Critic, A Logical Proposition (attributed to Bishop Beckwith), p. 2, Column 5, Logansport, In.

Distortions in our thinking negatively affect our words, actions, habits, and character without out being recognized. Counselors and psychologists help clients by examining their thinking for systematic errors that affect their relationships, jobs, decision making, and view of the world, of others, and of themselves. Sometimes, thinking errors are hard to discover.

Below is a list of common thinking errors, also called "cognitive distortions," a term coined by psychologist David Burns. Looking at this list can be helpful because, more likely than not, one or more are true of your thinking. And right now you have the choice to remain in comfortable sickness or to examine your thinking and grow.

Filtering

This cognitive distortion is characterized by someone who selectively pays attention to the negative but dismisses the positive. A few examples: a parent who only pays attention when their child acts out, ignoring all their good behavior; or a spouse who only pays attention when their partner overspends, ignoring all the times they stayed on budget.

Polarized Thinking (or "Black and White" Thinking)

This is when you perceive people, in the actions or words of others, or in the events of your own life, as being either good or bad, with no in-between. You put people in rigid categories of "good," "bad," "trustworthy," "heroic," or "dangerous."

Overgeneralization

This is when you take one fact and make it true of everything. For example, since one CEO took advantage of his company, we assume that all CEO's take advantage of their companies. Or, since someone from another race did something violent, we think everyone from that race is violent.

Jumping to Conclusions

The name of this cognitive distortion is fairly self-explanatory. This is when someone jumps to a conclusion before they have all the facts. You take a little bit of information and assume the rest.

Catastrophizing

This cognitive distortion is similar to overgeneralization but a little different, in that you take one thing that goes wrong and surmise that everything else in your life is also going wrong. For example, a woman fails at work and thinks that her relationship is going nowhere: so, no one loves her, she's unattractive and will never be successful in relationships.

Personalization

Personalization is when someone takes everything personally. In other words, they take what others say as a personal attack. For example, a dad tries to give his daughter feedback on her performance after a softball game. The daughter reacts to her dad as if he were critiquing her character. She felt like he was attacking her value and worth as a person when really he was trying to help her improve her performance.

Control Fallacies

Control fallacies have two sides, external and internal. *Externally*, we see our lives as totally controlled by outside forces- "There's nothing I can do to fix a problem or improve my life unless circumstances change." *Internally*, we take too much responsibility for what happens in the world and with others- "I'm at fault for everything that's gone wrong around me."

Fallacy of Fairness

This is the assumption that you should always be taken with, spoken of, and given fair treatment from others, while you ignore the fact that life isn't always fair. In a perfect world, this would not be a fallacy but a truth—but life is simply not fair. If we expect fair treatment all the time, we will constantly be disappointed.

Blaming

A person perceives their problems and struggles as the fault of another person, event, or circumstance while ignoring their own contribution to the problem. People ignore the log in their own eye while only seeing the speck in the other's.

Shoulds

"Shoulds" is the distorted thinking that assumes you or someone else ought to do something in a certain way. Morally speaking, there are "shoulds" and "oughts," but we can inappropriately label non-moral things with a moral level of conviction. Some examples of this cognitive distortion: assuming you should make a certain amount of money, assuming you should have a certain type of job, or assuming you should live in *this or that* kind of neighborhood.

Emotional Reasoning

This way of thinking assumes that what you feel must be true. Emotions reflect the way things truly are. This can be very misleading since emotions can change rapidly and aren't always based on what's true, but are sometimes based on our perceptions. This type of distortion runs the risk of censoring rational thought.

Fallacy of Change

We sometimes make our happiness and wellbeing contingent upon another person changing. The other person must change in order to suit me and have a relationship with me. This is an attempt to change others in such a way that satisfies our own desires.

Global Labeling

This error occurs when you take one aspect of yourself or your experience and generalize and misattribute it to the rest of your personality, character, and life. For example, you fail to complete a task at work satisfactorily, so you label yourself a "loser."

Always Being Right

The possibility of being wrong is ego-shattering. And so, you must always be right. You always have to prove your opinion and come out on top. This is a very limiting way of thinking since it eliminates the benefit of other's thoughts, opinions, and feedback.

Don't let unexamined thinking be the determinative force in your life. The process of exposing and examining the way we think gives us the space to correct faulty thinking and make changes. Otherwise, hidden faulty thinking will wreak havoc on our mental health. Understand, healthy thinking is a life-long job. As we mature in our thinking, we mature in all other aspects of our lives.

As a therapist, I see clients do the hard work of thought examination every day. It's not easy and can at times be very painful. People often misplace responsibility for their problems on others, failing to take responsibility for their own problematic thinking. This makes sense since one's thought life is the last place people look for problems. Yet, if you really want to live the best life you can, you need to be willing to humbly examine the areas where you need to grow—especially in your thinking patterns.

Take a moment and look over the cognitive distortions. Put a check mark next to the ones that you think are true of you. Then pick three which you think are the most problematic. This information provides you with an opportunity to do some personal work. Take out a journal, call a friend, or spend time in prayer. It doesn't matter what you do as long as you do something that helps you recognize your cognitive distortions. These four questions may help stimulate your thinking:

- What triggers my cognitive distortions?
- How does the cognitive distortion change the way I respond to my wife, son, or boss?
- Am I happy with how I respond?
- How could I respond more effectively?

Asking yourself these tough questions will allow you to be more aware of thinking distortions, how they affect you and those around you, and how you can work towards better thinking and responding. It's hard work, but it's worth it.

Learning to Forgive

Forgiveness is the oil of relationships.
Josh McDowell[11]

I'm sure you've heard the phrase "Forgive and forget." But is that really the best way to deal with hurt and forgiveness in your life? "Forgive and forget" can, for some, really mean "ignore and avoid." Ignoring or avoiding a problem can, for many reasons, be devastating to a relationship and to one's personal mental health. So, if this is you, listen up.

Two Ways We Get Forgiveness Totally Wrong

Forgiving an offense is a beautiful thing. It is powerful way to repair a broken bond. But forgiveness can also be tricky. It is easy to mess up forgiveness. One way we do this is when we withhold forgiveness when we shouldn't. Let me explain what I mean by that. Let's say your partner hurts you in a way that is uncharacteristic of them. They are normally very caring and thoughtful, but one time they acted selfishly. Okay, that's annoying, but very forgivable, right? It was a one-time thing. It's not reflective of who they are. We could call it a mistake, a lapse in judgment, or a one-off offense. But you shouldn't take a mistake as an indication of a person's character. Why? Character is something that is

---

[11] McDowell, Joshua (1999). *The One Year Josh McDowell's Youth Devotional*, Tyndale Kids, p. 241.

demonstrated over a lifetime. So, it's important to weigh someone's actions against what you know of their character. If someone hurts you and you are not familiar with their character, maybe hold off on the character assassination you want to commit. Don't jump to a conclusion about someone's character based on one or two examples. A one-time mistake is a forgivable offense, so forgive your partner, child, friend, or co-worker and move on.

It hurts when people create labels out of mistakes. I'm assuming you wouldn't like it if someone summed you up, life and character and all, based on one or two instances? When you forget something, for example, you don't want to be labeled as a forgetful person, right? When you knock over someone's beverage, you probably don't want to be labeled as a carless klutz, right? So, don't do it to others. When you do, it makes both giving and receiving forgiveness very difficult.

The second way we get forgiveness wrong is just the opposite. Instead of not forgiving for one-off offenses, we over-forgive for characteristic offenses. What do I mean by that? People tend to over-forgive relational offenses committed by those they love because *they are avoiding the truth about that person's character*. In other words, someone's actions are actually indicative of their character, but we don't want to believe that. They were thoughtless and selfish because they are a thoughtless and selfish person. I've seen this too many times in the counseling office to think it's an anomaly.

I remember working with a woman married to an abusive husband. She would often ask me, "Why does he act that way?" I had to bluntly explain to her that he acted abusively because he is an abusive person. His latest act of abuse wasn't a one-off thing. He had, for years, systematically berated, degraded, controlled, and beat his wife and kids. And yet, she forgave him every time. But she forgave not because she really believed he was sorry; she forgave him because she was in denial. Her denial allowed the abused to continue unabated.

Please don't misunderstand me. I'm not saying this woman was the cause for her own abuse or that she deserved it. No person has the right to abuse another person. No one should tolerate abuse. Abuse is wrong in any circumstance. There is no excuse. Lundy Bancroft, a therapist, author, and expert on abusive men once said, "When people conclude that anger causes abuse, they are confusing cause and effect." He then shares a story about a man that he worked with, Ray, that illustrates his point "Ray was not abusive because he was angry; he was angry because he was abusive. Abusers carry attitudes that produce fury."[12] My client's husband didn't abuse her because he was angry. He abused her because he was abusive. She was not the cause. But my client did carry some responsibility for what happened. Every time she forgave him and avoided change, the abuse continued.

The problem of over-forgiveness doesn't exist solely in cases of abuse; the same principle applies to different contexts. For example, I've seen a husband over-forgive his wife for being chronically unfaithful because he didn't want to face the implications of what her infidelity meant for their relationship. Did she have affairs because he wasn't enough? If he faced her

---

[12] Bancroft, Lundy (2003). *Why Does He Do That? Inside the Minds of Angry and Controlling Men*, Berkley Books, p. 37.

infidelity, would she leave him? And could he handle being alone? These thoughts and questions were so painful that he forgave her just to avoid the discomfort.

I've seen parents over-forgive their children because they don't want their kids to be unhappy with them. These parents aren't just "forgiving people." Rather, they forgive out of a desire for emotional approval from their kids.

I've discussed the problems with under-forgiveness and over-forgiveness— all the ways we get forgiveness wrong— but that leaves us with the question, what is healthy forgiveness?

Forgiveness and Change

Forgiveness is an act of grace, but it's also the first step in change. If your spouse, family member, parent, child, or friend made a mistake that isn't indicative of their character, then be generous and forgiving. Forgive them and move on. But, if your spouse, family member, parent, child, or friend has hurt you in a way that is indicative of their character; don't just let it go. Let forgiveness be the first step in change. So, how do you do this? When someone hurts you, follow the three A's of forgiveness:

Address: This first step involves bringing the grievance to the other person's attention. Share with them how their pattern of behavior affects you. Discuss their behaviors with them. Don't jump in with labels or judgements. Your goal is to be honest, but don't attack the other person. That will put them on the defensive and shutdown the communication process. You are sharing because you want the best for them and for the relationship.

Acknowledge: Forgiveness is a process between to people. In the first step, the wounded party addresses what happened, and how it made them feel. Then it is the responsibility of the offender to listen and acknowledge the effect their actions had on the other person. This can be hard to do, but acknowledge is essential in order for genuine forgiveness to happen. Just saying you're sorry does very little to repair the damage. Making an effort to understand the other person and then verbally acknowledging is very healing.

Action: At this point, the two parties can collaborate on what actions need to be taken to make an amends. The offender starts this process by asking "What can I do to make things right between us?" The wounded party may not have any ideas, and that's okay. Or they may have some specific actions in mind. This is a conversation. Not a lecture or instructions. This is a collaborative process between two people who both commit to new and healthy behaviors, attitudes, and mindsets. I encourage those who have been wounded, when asking the other to make changes, ask yourself what are ways that you can support the other in their behavior. Change can only happen when you work together.

The three A's of forgiveness are an incredibly helpful tool for relationships. They take bravery and consistency in use, but they can really help your relationship. Again, I wouldn't suggest using it for one-off offenses. Those are matters that can be discussed and forgiven quickly. But—when it comes to those people you fear or avoid for how they might respond or for fear of confronting their characteristic patterns—use those ABC's. That's when you need this tool the most. The choice is yours. But the alternative is an accumulation of relational damage over time, leading to disastrous results. I challenge you to practice the ABC's. Do so courageously. Do so lovingly. And do so consistently, even if you have to do it repeatedly for the same offense.

Learning to Set a Goal and Make It Happen

A goal properly set is halfway reached.

John Maxwell[13]

In 2008, the US economy was in freefall. In order to boost the nation's financial health, Congress signed into law a stimulus package that would give money to lower-middle class families. Researchers at the University of Miami and at the University of California, San Diego took the opportunity to test and examine how planning, saving money and self-control were affected among these families by the influx of extra cash.[14] Researchers wanted to see if test subjects were better able at saving their money and not overspending (i.e. exerting self-control) if they had a plan on how to use their money versus having no plan. In order to test this hypothesis, one group was given the stimulus package on the pre-condition that they develop a plan on how to use their money. The second group had no pre-condition, they were simply given the stimulus package.

After a period of time, the researchers measured the results of each group. Oddly enough, those who made a plan displayed poor self-control. Those who didn't

---

[13] Maxwell, John (2006). *Your Road Map for Success: You Can Get There From Here*, Thomas Nelson, p. 84.
[14] Townsend, Claudia, and Wendy Liu (2012). "Is Planning Good for You? The Differential Impact of Planning on Self-Regulation." *Journal of Consumer Research 39*, no. 4, 688-703.

make a plan had better self-control. It seemed that planning increased spending more than saving.

You might be saying to yourself, "Huh? You'd think planning ahead would help self-control, not hurt it." The reason those who planned exhibited poor self-control has nothing to do with the fact that they had a plan, but has everything to do with kind of plan they had. What researchers discovered is that those who planned, created unattainable goals relative to the money they were given. A goal that feels unattainable hurts motivation. Therefore, if you are putting out a great deal of effort, but feel as if you are not making progress on a goal, then you are more likely, in the case of money, lose motivation for saving and spend haphazardly.

What this study shows us is an insight that goes beyond spending habits. This study is very instructive for those who have goals for their life and want to be successful in achieving them. *How* you plan— setting goals, objectives and strategies— matters.

Being a counselor gives me a front-row seat to poor planning practices. I see clients setting themselves up for failure because of how they plan. That's where I lend some of my expertise in the goal-making phase.

So, what do I see them doing wrong? They make goals that are simply unattainable. These goals are big, far-reaching, and largely impractical. They want to change everything in their lives. Now, while I applaud them for ambitious goal-making, I want them to notice how overwhelming overly ambitious goals are. A goal that's overwhelming feels impossible, and impossible goals kill motivation. So, here are my quick and dirty tips for effective goal-making.

Take a Big Goal and Break it into Smaller Goals: This is a great antidote to the big-goal syndrome. If you want to change your life, ask yourself, "What parts of my life do I want to change? Weight loss? Relationships? Career goals?" Determine the different goal areas—careers, relationships, spirituality, etc. In one sentence, describe what you want. Then get specific with how you are going to achieve your goal. Let's say, for example, you want to lose weight. Please don't say you want to lose 200 pounds. Start with something attainable like two to five pounds. Then once you've gotten a win (i.e. you succeeded in losing 2–5 lbs.), then add to your goal by increasing the number to five to seven pounds, and so on. Losing two to five pounds is far more attainable than losing 200. With this method, too, you feel the positive satisfaction of getting a win. That win will motivate you to take on the next set of challenges. Building motivation is a journey, not an event. Start with small goals that are attainable, then work your way up to increasingly larger goals.

Make the Goal Measurable: I alluded to this next step in the weight-loss example above. If you choose a goal, make sure there is a way you can put some number to it. If you want to lose weight, you need to be specific—how much weight do you want to lose? Five pounds? Ten pounds? If you want to make more money—how much money? Doing this makes the goal feel real. People often make their goals vague. Pursuing a vague goal is like driving in thick fog. You think you're going the right way, but you have no clue if you're making progress or not because you can't see. Numbers help clear the fog. For instance, let's say you want to make a greater income next year, but you never put a number on it. So, you work really hard, harder than you have ever worked before, and you make a certain amount more. Did you make your goal? Maybe, maybe not. It's hard to tell without numbers. Instead of saying you want to make *more*, say you want to make $35,000 for example. So, you work hard and make $25,000. That's invaluable feedback! You were $10,000 short. This tells you there needs to be a change in your approach. It forces you to examine the reasons you didn't make your goal. The next year, you change your tactics. Instead of working "harder," you work "smarter" and end up making $40,000. Again, that's feedback. It tells you the adjustments you made worked.

Goals Must Be Realistic and Practical: An important key in goal-making is to be realistic and practical, and to consider what is within your control. In order for a goal to be realistic and practical, determine what you can functionally do. If you want to lose weight, there's only so much time you can dedicate to working out. If you have a job, a spouse, and kids, and a slew of other obligations in your life, working out several times a week for long periods of time may not be realistic and practical. So, set your goal relative to what you can realistically do. If you are only able to work out for 45 minutes three times a week, don't set a weight loss goal for losing 30 pounds in that time. But maybe you could lose five pounds in three weeks. That's a practical goal in light of what you can realistically accomplish given all your other life demands.

Goals and Controls: In order to accomplish a goal, the goal must be within your control. What do I mean by that? Changing another person *is not* within your control. However, changing how you respond to that person *is* within your control. So, don't make your goal dependent upon another person or situation changing. That simply leaves you stuck. Divide what you want into two categories: what is *within* your control and what is *outside* your control. Once you've done that, create attainable and measurable goals for what is within your control, and accept what is outside your control. You can't change what's outside your control, but you can change yourself.

After You've Set Your Goal, Make Objectives: The goal is what you want and objectives are how you plan on accomplishing the goal. Again, if your goal is to lose weight—well, how do you plan on losing weight? "I'll eat healthier" runs the risk of being vague. *How* do you plan on eating healthier? This is when you get down to monthly, weekly, daily, and hourly specifics. The more specific and concrete you can be, the more likely you are to follow through with your goal. For the goal of losing weight, a concrete objective could be to work out three times per week. You plan on only consuming 1,700 calories per day, and 1,100 of those calories will come from fruits and vegetables. That's concrete, specific, and measureable. If you worked out twice last week, you know you missed a day. If you consumed 2,200 calories yesterday, you know you over-ate by 500 calories. That feedback allows you to make the necessary adjustments to meet your objectives. If you're consistent with your objectives, you'll accomplish your goals.

Enlist Supporters, Friends and Partners in Your Goals: Don't lone-wolf your goals. If you think you can accomplish your goal alone, you are sorely mistaken. You need a community supporting and helping you. Community provides many benefits. Community gives you feedback, accountability, and encouragement. And trust me, when you are making some hard changes, you want people in your court. Setting and accomplishing a goal is incredibly hard work. It's life-changing. Don't do it alone. Supporters can help you when things get hard, lift your spirits when you've had setbacks, and celebrate your victories with you after a win. So, make sure to include your community in your goals.

Let's sum up. When you follow these steps we've discussed, one of the benefits is feeling the invigoration of a win. You need to feel "wins" along the way. I define a "win" as achieving a smaller goal while working on a bigger goal. That win makes you feel good and motives you to with what are doing. You feel like you can accomplish whatever you set your mind to. It also makes that "big" goal seem doable. Think back to the stimulus package recipients from 2008. Their goals were big, too big—goals that felt overwhelming and unattainable. However, if they felt like they were getting somewhere, additional planning wouldn't have killed their motivation and increased their spending. It would have been helpful.

Also, planning, goal setting, and determining objectives is best done with others. A goal set in isolation of a community is one destined for failure. Don't go the way of the lone wolf! Have a goal-buddy.

When you have help, encouragement, and assistance from others, a challenging goal becomes doable.

    I once worked with a middle-aged woman who was a bit of a recluse. She rarely left her mother's home. She struggled with social anxiety, and had a hard time meeting the demands of the workplace. Needless to say, she felt overwhelmed and hopeless. I started counseling her by asking a question: what did she want? She said she wanted to be a different person. I asked her to be more specific: what kind of person would she like to be? She gave me a long story that touched on three themes: she wanted to be someone who can talk comfortably with other people in a social setting, someone who could work consistently, and someone who lives on their own. As she was speaking, I wrote down three goals: work on easing social anxiety, live independently, and be confident at work. I read these back to her, and her eyes lit up. She said, "Yes, that's exactly what I want." Suddenly, this big ball of messy feelings, desires, and problems came untangled. She felt clarity on what she wanted and needed to do. From there, we determined what was in her control and what was outside her control. She spelled out specific, concrete, and measureable objectives. And I had her think of some people who could support her in reaching her goals. It was hard work at first, but after a few wins, she doubled her efforts. For her, the initial few wins were really the biggest wins. She, up to this point, felt like someone who couldn't accomplish anything. So, accomplishing any goal, small or big, was very important to her. It gave her a lot of confidence going forward. After some time, she landed a full-time job, started going out with friends, and eventually moved out of her mom's house.

This could be you. Don't let your problems feel like an overwhelming, unfixable mess. Untangle what you want into specific goals, create realistic and practical objectives, and get some support from friends. You'll be glad you did.

Learning the Importance of Feedback

A man convinced against his will, is of the same opinion still.

Dale Carnegie[15]

People see what they want to see. This is an old axiom often repeated, but is it true? Seeing, in the sense I'm talking about, has little to do with one's powers of eyesight. It's not about sight at all—it's about attention. We look for what we think we should see. Psychologists call this *selective attention*.

Attention has two sides. First, our brains are primed to look for the objects of our attention. Second, our brains dismiss all extraneous information. There's a famous example of this from researchers Daniel Simons and Christopher Chabris in their testing of self-awareness.[16] In their experiment, they ask participants to watch a video with several people in white and black clothing. They instruct the test subjects to count how many times a basketball is passed between the people wearing the white clothing. This is a bit demanding since everyone is moving around the frame and the people in black are passing basketballs, too. Then a person dressed in a gorilla suit walks through the scene. After the video is over, researchers interview

---

[15] Carnegie, Dale (2010), *How to Win Friends and Influence People*, Simon & Shuster, p. 123.
[16] Simons & Chabris (2004), *The Invisible Gorilla*, Harmony.

the test subjects on what they saw. The subjects reported the number of passes of the basketball, but when asked about the gorilla, they were clueless. They didn't notice the gorilla at all. The researchers showed them the video again, but this time told them to look for the gorilla. Test subjects were shocked because they hadn't seen the gorilla slowly walk through the frame. They couldn't believe they had missed it.

Why does something like this happen? Did the test subjects really not see the gorilla? The subjects did in fact *see* the gorilla, but they didn't *notice* the gorilla. Do you see the difference? Seeing and noticing are two different things. They saw the gorilla, but their attention was primed to look only for the basketball passes between the people wearing white, therefore their attention dismissed all extraneous information, like the gorilla. We see what we attend to and rule out everything else, which leaves us effectively blind to certain things. And because we have blind spots that entails we need other people . Others can catch what we miss. And if they care about us enough, they will offer feedback

You are capable of seeing, but are you capable of noticing? There's only so much you can notice. That's troubling to an extent, but what should really bother you is what you won't allow yourself to notice. Without realizing it, there are certain uncomfortable facts about yourself that you have dictated to your attention not to notice.

There are plenty of things in your life that point this out to you, but you won't allow yourself to notice them because you don't want to. This is called denial. Denial protects your ego, but keeps you from change.

Therefore, it is essential to have other people in your life who will point out such things, trusted friends who give you uncomfortable feedback for your benefit. You need people in your life who will make observations that raise your level of awareness so that you notice what you need to. You need other people to break your own denial.

Rejecting heartfelt and honest feedback damages relationships. This can be a relational killer. You must allow your trusted partner, friend, or family member to give you feedback. This is a difficult thing to do, especially when you disagree with them or when their feedback requires some kind of change in your life. Ask yourself these questions so that you don't dismiss their feedback too quickly. What evidences support their feedback? Are there reasons to back up what they are saying? Can others corroborate what they are saying? Is there a nagging sense in the back of your mind that they are right? If roles were reversed, would you say the same thing?

We need others' opinions in our lives. As history (along with the most current social science) has borne out, people can have serious blind spots, especially when it comes to their own character, decision-making, and opinions. A good leader, for example, is leery of surrounding themselves with "yes-men." If you are surrounded by people who only tell you what you want to hear, you're handicapping yourself. Critical feedback is vital for personal growth. Don't allow your selective attention to cancel out your own growth. Listen to those whom you trust and who have your interests at heart, those who provide feedback for the sake of your own growth.

Mutual Influence

Receiving feedback is essential for personal growth. It is also essential for relational health. It is a key component in the trust between intimate partners. That means feedback is a two-way street. You must open yourself up to giving feedback with the goal of positively influencing the other person for their benefit and receiving feedback for your own.

Let me give you an example of how feedback played a critical role for a couple I worked with. Some time ago I was speaking with client on whether she should do counseling or not. She didn't see the need to do counseling, but she was willing to do it in order to prove to her husband that she didn't have a problem. She asked if this was a good reason to do counseling. I explained in no uncertain terms that this was not a good reason to do counseling. She didn't respond. I then said she would benefit from having her blind spots exposed, which would help her avoid problematic traps in her relationship. She thought this was meaningless counselor jargon and didn't respond. What I said next shaped the course of our future sessions. I said that if it doesn't matter to her but it does matter to the ones she cares about, then it's worth doing. She thought for a moment and admitted that was a good enough reason to try. She started counseling and working on her relationship. I think about this conversation often. And one question keeps emerging in my mind: shouldn't this idea guide us throughout marriage and not just in times of crisis?

Too often, we dismiss the opinions of those closest to us. But this doesn't make sense, does it? Why wouldn't we listen to those most invested in our lives? Why wouldn't we listen to those who care the most about us? Why wouldn't we listen to those who have a vested interest in our wellbeing? Why wouldn't you be willing to change for that person? Of course, if your spouse is asking you to become a drug dealer, terrorist, or contract killer, don't change for them. Yet, if your spouse is asking you to be more consistent, become a better listener, follow a budget, back them up on parenting choices, pick up after yourself, or stop a pet peeve, then do it. Even though you may disagree with what they are saying, if the person is of value to you, then you should value what is important to them.

In no way, do I think this is an easy thing to do, even though this it seems like common sense. You wouldn't believe how many couples I've counseled who struggle with this idea. The reason is that valuing what the other person values might require change.

My client's husband wasn't willing to continue the relationship because he viewed her behavior as abusive. The client strongly disagreed. If she wanted to keep her marriage, she needed to reevaluate her behavior. This, as you can imagine, was a difficult thing to do. She asked me again why she should do this. I repeated what I said to her before: "If it matters to those who matter to you, then do it." And I added, "Out of all the people we must change for, why not your spouse?" We must change our behavior for co-workers, bosses, family members, and friends—but when it comes down to spouses, we throw a fit and refuse?

How does that make sense? She said my advice was a bitter pill to swallow, but it made sense.

So, here are a few ways in which you can practice the idea of valuing what matters to those who matter to you:

- Show interest in what your partner is interested in.
- Listen to their feedback on your behavior.
- Pay attention to their stressors and stress relievers.
- Validate their feelings.
- Encourage and support their dreams.
- Give them feedback on how their behavior affects you.

Be open to feedback. Acknowledge the fact that you are limited by your perceptions. Acknowledge the fact that you could be wrong. Listen carefully to the feedback of others, especially when it comes from people you trust and have your best interests in mind. Listen hard especially when their feedback makes you uncomfortable. Don't dismiss them outright simply because you disagree. Take some time and consider what they said. And take the risk to give your partner feedback as well. Not sharing is just as bad as not listening. Follow this advice. It may just save your marriage, relationship, family, or job.

Learning About Abusive Relationships and What to Do if You're in One

> But whether you stay or go, the critical decision you can make is to stop letting your partner distort the lens of your life, always forcing his way into the center of the picture. You deserve to have life be about you; you are worth it.
>
> Lundy Bancroft[17]

I'm a therapist who has worked with women, children, and even abusers in domestic violence and abuse (DVA) situations. These are never easy cases to work with. Often I walk away from sessions feeling hopeless and worried for the victims—but not for the reasons you might think.

I don't feel hopeless as if the situation truly has no solution. And I don't feel hopeless as if the abuser really has all the power.

I feel hopeless because abused men and women fail to understand something absolutely vital: *they fail to recognize that they are not powerless!* They are not worthless, and they do not deserve the treatment they are getting. What is happening to them is unequivocally wrong! And, most importantly, they are not at fault for the abuse they are receiving. Unfortunately, abused partners often don't understand this.

---

[17] Bancroft, Lundy (2003) *Why Does He Do That? Inside the Minds of Angry and Controlling Men*, Berkley Books, p. XIV.

They have bought into their abuser's *lies*. They believe they are the cause of their mistreatment. They believe they are lucky to have anyone show them attention, and they'd better be grateful for what they have, even if the attention is abusive. They think they are weak, powerless, and unintelligent, and that they shouldn't bother family and friends with their problems. But these beliefs are based on a lie created by the abuser. An abused partner is controlled to the degree that he or she buys their abuser's lies. Understanding the role of control in abuse provides insight for why abusers do what they do. Lundy Bancroft is an expert on domestic violence and abuse. He's done groundbreaking research on abusive men. He has spent years treating abusers and has written several books on the subject. He once said regarding control,

> "When a man starts my program, he often says, 'I am here because I lose control of myself sometimes. I need to get a better grip.' I always correct him: 'Your problem is not that you lose control of yourself, it's that you take control of your partner. In order to change, you don't need to gain control over yourself, you need to let go of control of her.'"[18]

Something you need to understand is that when Bancroft speaks of abusers, he always refers to men. And when he speaks of victims, he always speaks of women. This is not because he's being prejudicial. This is supported by the numbers. The vast majority of

---

[18] Ibid, p. 54.

abusers are men, and the vast majority of abuse victims are women. There's no question about that. However, there are more recent statistics coming forward revealing a growing number of men being abused by their female partners.[19] So, that is why I refer to victims of abuse in gender-neutral terms. Bancroft also rightly identifies control as being the central issue in DVA. The abuser feeds off control of another. And in order to control another person, you have to tear them down.

If you are a victim of abuse, it is critical for you to understand that, in order to take back your life, you have to take responsibility for your part in believing the abuser's lies. Your abuser needs you to believe they are in control. Your abuser has crossed the line so many times you've lost count. They've lied, cheated, hit, cursed, and intimidated. You know deep down that you should have left a hundred times by now, but you didn't. You didn't because you rationalized, minimized, and falsely believed you were powerless. When you take responsibility for your part, you take back control.

No, your abuser should not have been abusive. Those things were wrong. But, at the same time, you need to take responsibility for the mental and emotional gymnastics you did to justify staying with them or not standing up to them. I write this empathically because I have worked with women who stay and don't stand up for themselves because they are afraid of punishment and other forms of abuse, and because they fear for their kids' safety,. I get it. It's hard to leave. There are a million reasons to stay, but

---

[19] The National Domestic Violence Hotline
http://www.thehotline.org/2014/07/men-can-be-victims-of-abuse-too/ Retrieval: December, 28th, 2015.

ignoring or dismissing the abuse only allows it to continue. If you change nothing, nothing will change.

Please, do not misunderstand what I say. I am not blaming the victim. I want DVA victims to feel empowered. And I think the only way to do that is by rightly acknowledging the abuser's actions as wrong and identifying how the abuser's power rests on your belief in their lies. Victims must start thinking strategically about how to leave, how to protect themselves and their kids, how stand up to their abuser, and how to understand their part in accepting the abuser's lie that they are powerless.

I've worked with so many victims to whom I've asked simple questions like, "Have you called Child Protective Services? Have you called the police? Have you tried to leave? Are there people you trust and can stay with? Do you have a safety plan? Have you challenged your abusive partner's behavior instead of accepting or forgiving it? Have you shared with them how hurtful their behavior is? Have you asked your partner to see a counselor?" Often, they look at me bewildered because these questions have never come into their mind. And this is because they never considered that change could happen in their situation. But *change is possible.*

As you can imagine, working with victims (women, men, and children) in DVA situations is an uphill battle. But those who have been successful made small changes over time to regain power. And this is how they did it:

- Rejecting the lie of powerlessness.
- Reestablishing ties with family and friends.

- Sharing their story.
- Making a safety plan.
- Gathering supporters and allies around them, not combatants against the abuser.
- Creating independence by getting a job, creating their own checking account, and finding support groups.
- Leaving if they need to. On average, it takes an abuse victim six attempts before they successfully leave the home.
- No longer making excuses for their abuser.
- Learning to challenge their abuser's behavior while maintaining personal safety.
- Stopping rationalization of domestic violence and abuse. It is wrong and it needs to stop.

Know, in your heart of hearts, you do not deserve abuse! It is not normal. Relationships are built on trust, love, and self-sacrifice, not on selfishness, violence, manipulation, and control. Stop believing the lie that you are powerless—you are stronger than you think! Domestic violence and abuse is wrong and should never be tolerated. Be willing to call the cops or proper authorities. There is help. Be willing to take it.

If you are in an abusive relationship, it is my hope this chapter has given you courage and empowerment. Thousands of abuse victims have learned to stand up to their abusers. Thousands of abuse victims have successfully left their abusive partners. Change is possible. A better life is out there. Others have done it, and so can you!

Learning to Recognize the Patterns and Roles that Hurt Your Family

> Families are messy…Sometimes the best we can do is to remind each other that we're related for better or for worse…and try to keep the maiming and killing to a minimum.
>
> Rick Riordan[20]

I've worked with many families that get caught in destructive patterns of behavior they can't break. More than likely you've experienced dysfunction in your family of origin or in your current family situation. But when sit and try to think of what those patterns are, they may be hard to identify. These patterns are hard to recognize for two big reasons.

First, identifying how your family functions— patterns of behavior, relational dynamics, family norms and values— can be hard to do because the way your family operates is how you define normal. Family is the lens through which we see everything else.

Second, families are uncomfortable facing destructive patterns. Therefore, the focus shifts to one

---

[20] Riordan, Rick (2013). *Demigods and Monsters: Your Favorite Authors on Rick Riordan's Percy Jackson and the Olympians Series,* Smart Pop, p. 115.

member. This one person receives all the blame for what everyone is experiencing. Don't buy what I am saying? That's fine! I have examples (and I must be right if I have examples).

Families operate as a system of interconnected parts. Each part affects another part, kind of like a chain reaction. For example, when you throw a stone in a pond, ripples spread across the water and affect the fish and plant life. Or think about how a Newton's cradle operates—you know, the pendulum thing with the metal balls. You lift the ball at one end and let go. That creates a chain reaction. Okay, one more (I'm on a roll now). Let's say you're playing pool. You strike the cue ball to break, which propels other pool balls across the table. The entire configuration of pool balls has changed because of what that one ball did. Families function in a similar way. One person's actions, attitudes, or words affect everyone else. And how one person responds to another, could either fix the problem or perpetuate it. Depending on how people react, the problem could continue and get worse or stop. Put another way, one action gives rise to another, like in a feedback loop. Therefore, everyone in a family has a part to play in the problem. I'll say that again: each person is responsible for their contribution to the problem. No one is blameless, and no one is totally guilty.

So, why does the blame usually land on one person? Why are so many families blind to the pattern they're all participating in? The reason is that dysfunction in families is deeply shameful. And people don't like to talk about, acknowledge, or admit to shame. And so, toxic family patterns— the kinds that tear people down, create addiction, increase mental illness, or lead to suicide—continue unchecked. Usually, the person brave or foolish enough to draw attention to the toxic pattern also draws blame and negativity. But why does that happen? Shouldn't this person be considered a hero? It happens for three reasons.

First, toxic family patterns, in addition to being shameful, are secretive. And, if the secret were ever let out, the family would be forced to change. In other words, secrets foster denial. Denial, for many, is comfortable. It doesn't require you to change. And change is scary. Families get so used to their toxic patterns, they're actually afraid to give them up, even when the pattern causes serious damage.

Second, members of a dysfunctional family adapt to their toxic pattern in such a way that they can sometimes derive a kind of benefit from it. Psychologists call this *secondary gain*. Imagine, if you will, a father who has been chronically drunk for years. And when Dad is heavily drunk, he beats his son. But Dad only binge drinks when his son is defiant. Oddly enough, the family can't go a week without the son acting out, leading Dad to binge drink and beat him. Why would the son create or support a situation in which he gets beat? After Dad beats his son, he's exhausted and passes out on his recliner for the rest of the night. This allows the son to leave, hang out with his friends, meet up with girls, smoke weed, and engage in other risky behavior without adult supervision or accountability. In the son's mind, this is a bargain. For fifteen minutes of beating, he gets total freedom. That is a secondary gain.

The third reason for blame being directed at one person concerns family roles. Roles unconsciously dictate behavior and responses. Roles are very powerful and can feed into destructive family patterns. There are five roles that people typically play in dysfunctional families:

The Hero: The hero role is played by someone in the family who, despite the struggles, has risen above. He or she is someone on whom the family pins their hopes, dreams, and aspirations. If the hero can make it in the world, then their family wasn't all that bad. If something goes right, it's the hero's doing. The hero can rescue the family from the problem or distract them from it.

The Scapegoat: This family member gets blamed for all that's wrong with the family. If something goes wrong, it's the scapegoat's fault.

The Symptom-Bearer: This family member bears all the stress, hurt, and emotional damage of the family. The family doesn't speak about what's going on, but the effects can be manifestly seen in the symptom-bearer. Often, the person who plays this role is sick, has psychosomatic disorders, or struggles with addiction.

The Lost One: The lost one is emotionally or physically distant from the family. They make their best effort to be unseen and unheard. They often blame the family's dysfunction on themselves, much like the symptom-bearer, and in an attempt to help, they remove or avoid drawing attention to themselves.

The Court Jester: This family member is a performer. Their role is to distract the family from what's really going on. When there has been a big upset, the court jester makes everyone feel better by breaking the tension, which helps everyone forget what just happened.

Can you guess which role gets all the blame in dysfunctional families? That's right, you guessed it, the scapegoat. Dysfunctional families direct all the blame, negativity, and focus on the scapegoat. They are convenient targets to vent all the family's anger, hurt and tension.

Family roles are also a problem because they perpetuate family dysfunction. How do they do that?

Typically, there are one or two people playing some of the roles listed above. It is unusual to see all the roles played out, but I once worked with such a case. I'm not kidding. Here's a quick rundown on the family: Dad was the court jester. He was also physically abusive. So, in order to lighten the mood after he abused his family, he shared funny stories, cracked jokes, and tried to pass his abuse off as if it were a joke. The oldest son was the hero. He moved out of the home. He went to college, got good grades, and started working at a successful firm. His achievements were often the focal point of many family discussions. Dad would often say that he couldn't be "*that* bad" since the oldest son was doing so well. The successes of the oldest made everyone feel good. The youngest son received all the blame for all the family problems. The way Dad put it, the youngest forced him to physical abuse because his behavior was so disrespectful. Mom was the symptom-bearer. She felt paralyzed by her husband's terror over the family. She wanted to protect her son, but she didn't know how. That pain and stress manifested as an anxiety disorder. Even though she was on medication, it didn't help. She wouldn't leave the house or her room for days on end. In this way, she played a second role, the lost one. Collectively, everyone was terrified to discuss what was really going on. If the outside world knew what really went on in their house, it would be incredibly shameful and embarrassing. Individually, everyone was doing their best to make the problem better, but as a whole, living out their roles and remaining silent only disguised and perpetuated the destructive family pattern.

As I said before, destructive family patterns are shameful and secretive; they perpetuate themselves by secondary gains and force people into unhealthy roles. If your family is caught in a destructive pattern, there is hope. Change is possible. It has been said, you are as sick as your secrets. The secrets you keep as a family have the potential to suffocate your emotional health. Breaking the silence and facing what's really going on is the path forward. Here are my six steps on how to do that:

Change Your Focus: Break free from individual blame and look at how the whole family participates in the problem. Everyone plays a part in what doesn't work.

Recognize What Role You Play in the Problem: Which family role do you play? How does your role perpetuate the problem? What can you do differently?

Speak the Unspeakable: Don't let shame keep you in silence. Is maintaining the secret worth perpetuating the pain? Denial keeps your family stuck.

If No One Will Listen, Change How You Respond: You cannot change another person, but you can change how you respond to the pattern. By not going along with the destructive pattern or playing your role, you force change. Remember, the family is an interconnected system. If one part starts acting differently, that has an effect on the whole.

Be Patient: Family systems are like government bureaucracies. They can be slow and resistant to change. So, be patient and give it time.

Be Steadfast: If you decide to break away from the family norm, expect resistance. People don't like change and your family will want you to act in ways like how you have behaved before. Despite the pushback, be consistent with healthy ways of living. You will be tempted to fall back into old patterns, but don't give in. Change will come.

Learning to Be Proactive So You Don't Have to Be Reactive

Look at the word responsibility—"response-ability"—the ability to choose your response. Highly proactive people recognize that responsibility. They do not blame circumstances, conditions, or conditioning for their behavior. Their behavior is a product of their own conscious choice, based on values, rather than a product of their conditions, based on feeling.

Stephen Covey[21]

Reactivity is the willful ignorance of a problem. When that ignorance is confronted with the truth, a person becomes defensive, rude, irrational, or argumentative. The reactive person will openly deny the problem, change the subject, cast blame on others, or shut down. Why do people do this? How can people behave so illogically? The answer, simply put, is fear. People are afraid because facing a problem requires change. So, it's easier to pretend like the problem isn't there. The fear of change, accompanied by the denial of a problem, forces a

---

[21] Covey, Stephen R. (2013). *The 7 Habits of Highly Effective People: Powerful Lessons in Personal Change* (25th Anniversary Edition), Rosetta Books, Kindle Location 1520-1523.

person into a reactive way of thinking and behaving. And being in a reactive position comes with some serious disadvantages.

The Disadvantages of Being Reactive

Ignoring a problem allows it to mutate into a worse problem. For example, couples, on average, tend to engage counseling services seven years after a problem has been going on.[22] Seven years! That's a long time to live with a problem. Relationally speaking, that period of time allows resentment, bitterness, and hurt to build up to a point where no solution will work. *We make problems worse when we ignore them.*

Let's say someone loves you enough to confront you, and instead of listening, you become reactive. You try to deny what they're saying, you accuse them of projecting their problems on you, or you bring up all their problems to direct attention away from you. Doing this will lead to serious personal damage. Relationships don't thrive when feedback cannot be freely and safely exchanged.

Finally, all the time and energy you spend ignoring and denying the problem is time you could have spent working on the solution. I've heard many clients share deep regret for not seeking counseling earlier in their lives. They are ashamed of how long they lived in denial and how many years were wasted when they could have been enjoying their lives. *The discomfort of change is a small price to pay for living a life free of fear*

---

[22] https://www.gottman.com/blog/timing-is-everything-when-it-comes-to-marriage-counseling/. Retrieval: January, 22nd, 2016.

and reactivity. Don't live a life of reactivity. Learn this hard lesson and become proactive.

Proactive

The proactive person respects themselves, their relationships, their families, their jobs, and their communities enough to not waste time and resources when it comes to problems. If someone confronts a proactive person with a legitimate concern, they engage in what the other is saying. They don't allow their ego to blind them to the truth. In other words, the proactive person is humble enough to recognize that they're not perfect and that they have weaknesses—even weaknesses they may not be able to see. The proactive person is, therefore, open to the opinions of trusted friends who can see what they cannot. If you want to be a proactive person, you need the involvement of others in your life. You need the kind of people who will love you enough to say the hard things.

Stewardship

Proactive people are good stewards of what they have. They tend to their relationships, jobs, and mental health like gardeners tend to their gardens. This means you have to be observant. You have to be watchful for weeds creeping into your life. I know many couples who do maintenance sessions with a therapist once every year. They do this habitually, not because of a crisis, but because they want to stay on the right track. They want to celebrate their strengths and nip problems at the bud. This may seem odd to do, but think about it for a moment. You're supposed to see your dentist every six months for a cleaning. You're supposed to visit the doctor for a flu shot every year. You take your car in for a maintenance check at the mechanic. We all accept these annual, sometimes biannual or more, obligations without much protest. So why don't you perform similar maintenance when it comes to your relationships and mental health? The maintenance way of thinking seems completely normal for our physical health, but when it comes to our mental or relational health, the idea seems bizarre. Why? Why do we distinguish between our physical health and our mental health? Why do we take our physical health so seriously, but ignore our mental, emotional, and relational needs?

Ask for Help When You Need it

Proactive people realize they are not alone when battling against a problem. I've heard it said that it takes a village to raise child. Well, I think the same thing goes for tackling a mental-health, relational, or family problem. You need a village to help in times of crisis and struggle. You need other people to lend their expert advice, to give a listening ear or a shoulder to cry on. So, don't be afraid to ask for help when you need it.

Unfortunately, in our culture, people who access counseling, psychiatry, and therapy services are thought of as "crazy," are viewed as weak, broken, or damaged. And so, the people who need mental health services don't access them because they are afraid of the negative associations. There is tremendous pressure to "fit in" and be viewed as "normal."

The sad reality is that these negative cultural associations create a stigma around mental illness. Stigma makes a widely felt and experienced issue, a hidden issue. It is time to take mental illness out of the shadows. Here are a few facts from the National Institute of Mental Health (NIMH) to show how prevalent mental illness is among the US population:

- "Approximately 1 in 5 adults in the U.S.—43.8 million, or 18.5%—experiences mental illness in a given year.[23]
- Approximately 1 in 25 adults in the U.S.—10 million, or 4.2%—experiences a serious mental illness in a given year that substantially interferes with or limits one or more major life activities.[24]
- Approximately 1 in 5 youth aged 13–18 (21.4%) experiences a severe mental disorder at some point during their life. For children aged 8–15, the estimate is 13%."[25]

More than likely, you or someone you know (like a family member or friend) has been diagnosed or at one point has struggled with a mental health disorder. The truth is, mental illness is, in fact, normal. It is normal to struggle. The standard by which we judge others should not be whether or not someone struggles, but

---

[23] Any Mental Illness (AMI) Among Adults. (n.d.). Retrieved October 23, 2015, from http://www.nimh.nih.gov/health/statistics/prevalence/any-mental-illness-ami-among-adults.shtml

[24] Serious Mental Illness (SMI) Among Adults. (n.d.). Retrieved October 23, 2015, from http://www.nimh.nih.gov/health/statistics/prevalence/serious-mental-illness-smi-among-us-adults.shtml

[25] Any Disorder Among Children. (n.d.) Retrieved January 16, 2015, from http://www.nimh.nih.gov/health/statistics/prevalence/any-disorder-among-children.shtml

whether or not they choose to seek help, whether or not they choose to overcome their issues by facing them. We ought to have compassion for those who struggle with mental illness. It is possible that, at some point, you will struggle with a mental illness. At that point, would you want someone judging you or helping you? How would you want to be treated?

I'm going to get on my soapbox here for a moment. I think proactive people feel compassion for themselves and for others. They know how to advocate for their own needs or the needs of others. Being an advocate doesn't mean you have to become a lawyer or give some organization your life-savings. There are simple, small, daily things you can do to help. The first is to not allow yourself to judge others based on their mental illness. This may be the hardest step of all. But when you see someone on the street acting odd, panhandling, wearing grubby clothes, or talking to themselves, ask yourself, "What if that were my dad? What if that were my son? What if that were my friend?" You wouldn't mock them, would you? No, you'd probably try to help them, or at the very least, you wouldn't judge them. Secondly, when others are making critical and judgmental comments about another person based on their mental illness, be gently subversive by making the suggestion that those are people; people who have value; people who are struggling; people who have families and stories, and who are deserving of human decency. Third, change your language. Language shapes the way people think. So, if you refer to someone with a mental illness as "crazy," a "nut job," "psycho," or "lunatic," that perpetuates negative cultural associations. However, if your language communicates compassion, understanding, and respect, then those messages and associations are perpetuated. And slowly, the negative associations will change.

Seek Help Early

When a proactive person can humbly listen to the feedback of a trusted friend and admit they need outside help, they act quickly. They won't settle for a life of denial. They seek help early. When you seek help early, you are giving yourself, your family, your marriage, your job, and your own wellbeing a fighting chance. Otherwise, the damage only increases and the problem worsens. A problem is far easier to fix early in its life. However, if you ignore a problem, it gets bigger, meaner and tougher to fix.

Hopefully, you are sufficiently convinced to become a proactive person. That isn't to say it's easy to become one. In fact, it's not easy at all, but the benefits far outweigh the disadvantages. Being proactive is the willingness to no longer live in fear. It is the desire to no longer have your life ruled by reactivity. So, reclaim your life, face your problems, ask for help, rely on the support of others, and don't live in regret.

Learning the Connection Between Spirituality and Health

> Just as a candle cannot burn without fire, men cannot live without a spiritual life.
>
> Buddha[26]

Want to be healthy? Want to live a long, satisfying life? Do you want your body to stay in the best condition for as long as possible? If you answered yes to any of these questions, then you might be interested to know that physical health is closely connected with spiritual health. Health and longevity researchers have discovered an undeniable relationship between the two. If religion has always turned you off, or if faith plays a minor role in your life, or if spirituality is something you've never explored, don't skip this chapter. You don't have to be deeply religious to access the benefits of a spiritual lifestyle.

Research of Religiosity

---

[26] Demakis, Joseph (2014). *The Ultimate Book of Quotations*, p. 431. Kindle Edition.

The majority of Americans (90%) believe there is a God or a higher power. 75% pray on a daily basis, 69% are members of a church or synagogue, 40% of the US population attends a church or synagogue regularly, 60% acknowledge religion as very important in their lives, and 82% recognize a need for spiritual growth.[27] Faith, religion, and spirituality are without a doubt an essential part of the American landscape. Furthermore, Americans recognize the intersection of spirituality with their overall health. Over 75% of healthcare consumers want their physicians to include spiritual issues in their healthcare. Around half of Americans want their physicians to consult them on religious matters and even to pray with them.[28]

Doctors, medical and mental health practitioners, and professional groups are starting to pay attention to the importance of spirituality. More, funds are being directed to research and more conferences and symposia are being held to better understand the role of spirituality in healthcare than ever before.

So, what are some findings discovered from this new research focus? Study after study has found a connection between religious involvement and decreased rates in overall health problems and mortality. For example, high religious involvement may be associated with up to seven years of increased life expectancy. Another research study reported that on average 91,000 people in a Maryland county who attended church regularly had lower rates of cirrhosis,

---

[27] Andrew Newberg, *Measuring the Immeasurable: The Scientific Case for Spirituality*, Sounds True, p. 357
[28] Ibid, p. 357

emphysema, suicide, and death from ischemic heart disease.[29] Other studies have found that a high rate of involvement with a church has a beneficial effect on blood pressure. These results can be mitigated by a number of socioeconomic factors, including geography and access to health care. Yet the link between religious involvement and positive health benefits is undeniable.[30]

There are also surprising findings from disease and surgical outcomes research that demonstrate the power of religious commitment in a person's life. In a study of 232 patients following elective open heart surgery, the patient's level of commitment and support from a faith community was a consistent predictor of survival. In a different study that followed patients after heart surgery, stronger religious beliefs were associated with faster recovery time, shorter hospital stays, and fewer medical complications.[31] A study that looked at recovery time from spinal surgery found the same results. One study that looked at elderly women after hip repair surgery found that religious beliefs were associated with fewer symptoms of depression and a greater ability to walk. There are groups of studies that do not show statistically significant effects of religiousness on treatment outcomes, particularly ones which looked at people with cancer. However, the data does show that religious commitment does have a positive effect on the way a person copes and recovers from disease, including cancer.

---

[29] Ibid, p. 358
[30] Ibid, p. 359
[31] Ibid, p. 359

The claim that faith, religious involvement, and spirituality benefits physical health is firmly supported by the evidence—but how do they impact mental health and wellbeing?

Across the globe, people from differing ethnic, cultural, and socioeconomic situations experience mental health and wellbeing benefits from faith, religious involvement, and spirituality. Among white American, Mexican-American, and African-American populations, religiousness is positively associated with feelings of wellbeing. Furthermore, religious service attendance is predictive of higher life satisfaction among elderly Chinese Hong Kong residents and elderly Mexican-American women. In Israel, members of religious Kibbutzes reported a higher sense of coherence and less hostility, and were found more likely to engage in volunteer work than nonmembers. Similar results occurred in a population of nursing home residents. There are also higher levels of hope and optimism in religious than non-religious populations. From these findings, we can conclude that, globally, higher religious commitment, belief, and involvement are associated with higher levels of hope, optimism, wellbeing, and prosocial activities.[32]

What has been presented above is only a fraction of the existing research which links religiosity with physical and mental wellbeing. To reiterate, researchers have found a positive correlation between religiosity and positive behavior, lifestyle changes and habits, improved depression, enhanced coping, and resistance to medical problems. Across the board, religious involvement and higher levels of religiosity

---
[32] Ibid, p. 363

are associated with multiple markers of health and wellbeing.

In cases of spiritual abuse— overly rigid, inflexible, and fundamentalist religious involvement— the findings concerning people who forego medical treatment for strictly spiritual interventions such as prayer and religious healing are not positive.[33] Yet, most religious people would readily admit these are extreme aspects of religion and are not considered the norm. Understanding this potential for abuse, many recognize that the good outweighs the negative.

Faith, religious involvement, and spirituality can also have observable organic benefits to an individual's neurological functioning. In other words, spirituality helps your brain.

Research of Spiritual Practices

Spirituality can be beneficial for brain health.[34] When a person is meditating, for example, the meditator can experience a very intense feeling of joy or a state of bliss. The brain system associated with the feeling of joy is the sympathetic nervous system. The brain system associated with the state of bliss is a quiescent reaction from the parasympathetic nervous system. In some cases, people have reported having a profound mystical experience when both systems are activated: an ecstatic state of bliss. Some psychopharmacological studies have found that during meditation and prayer, there is an increase in dopamine (the body's natural reward/pleasure neurotransmitter) and a decrease in

---

[33] Ibid, p. 360
[34] Ibid, p. 354

the hypothalamus' production of cortisol (the body's stress hormone). Researchers have found positive effects in the body's immune system from decreased levels of cortisol.[35]

The parasympathetic and sympathetic systems are two key systems in your central nervous system. They are important systems in your body to keep you healthy and happy. Meditation, prayer, and contemplation, deeply spiritual practices, help your brain soothe and release stress while making you feel good and motivated. Let's take a deeper look at some of these practices.

Meditation

Meditation has become very common in the treatment plans of doctors and psychotherapists. It is often recommended to heart disease, arthritis, and anxiety patients. Studies have shown meditation to have many beneficial effects on a person's health, such as achieving a state of restful alertness with improved reaction time, creativity, and comprehension, and decreases in anxiety, depression, irritability, and moodiness. These effects, in turn, improve learning ability, memory, sense of self-actualization, feelings of vitality and rejuvenation, and emotional stability.

Other studies have shown that meditation benefits, stabilizes, and decreases pain for patients with chronic disorders such as hypertension, psoriasis, irritable bowel syndrome, anxiety, depression, and fibromyalgia. Some studies have found that meditators

---

[35] Ibid, p. 355

even have lower cholesterol levels and better lung and heart functioning than non-meditators.

Prayer

One-fourth of Americans, according to one of the largest alternative medicine surveys, use prayer to cope with a physical illness. Some studies have shown that prayer may be associated with a range of physical benefits, such as reduced muscle tension, improved cardiovascular and neuroimmunological parameters, psychological, physical, and spiritual peace, a greater sense of purpose, enhanced coping skills, less disability, better physical function in patients with knee pain, and lower incidence of coronary heart disease. Prayer has also been found to decrease levels of depression, anxiety, and stress among individuals.[36]

Yoga

Yoga, a widely used practice, predates Hinduism and is not tied to any particular religious doctrine. It has been accepted by practitioners of many different religions, including Christians, as a helpful form of exercise. Yoga is based on the premise that a person's body has a flow of life force: pain and disease enters the body when the life force is blocked. Stretching, breathing, and relaxation techniques help to release these blockages and allow the life force to flow. Clinical studies have shown reduced serum total cholesterol, LDL cholesterol, triglyceride levels, and improved pulmonary function in yoga practitioners. Use of yoga

---
[36] Ibid, p. 367

is also associated with acute and long-term decreases in blood pressure, and may benefit patients with asthma, hypertension, heart failure, mood disorders and diabetes. Two small controlled studies have demonstrated that Hatha Yoga, a form of yoga that develops mental and physical strength through postures and exercises, can significantly alleviate pain in osteoarthritis of the fingers and carpal tunnel syndrome.[37]

Keep Spiritual and Practical Needs in Balance

As you've read, a substantial body of scientific research supports the idea that faith, religious involvement, spirituality, and spiritual practices benefit physical and mental health. So, if you truly want to be a physically and mentally healthy person, you can't ignore the spiritual dimension to life. Spirituality is essential to physical health. Therefore, you may want rebalance your life to include your spiritual needs. Here are a few suggestions on how to do that:

Join a Faith Community: Find a group that meets regularly for the purpose of connecting and supporting each other. Look for a group that loves each other, connects with a story bigger than their own, and wants to do good, and encourages your personal and spiritual growth.

Pray Every Day: Prayer should not be intimidating. Prayer is a peaceful internal place where you can express yourself with the divine presence in your life.

---
[37] Ibid, p. 368

Share your struggles, victories and needs. It's that simple.

Read Scripture: Find a scripture that inspires, convicts, strengthens, and encourages you. Read it on a consistent basis. This doesn't have to be a major commitment. 10-15 minutes is all you need, and if you want to read more, then go for it!

Live Life with a Purpose: Your life is about more than just you. Your story fits within a larger narrative. Your life has significance and a purpose. Whatever purpose that is, align your words, actions, and thoughts with it. It will give you a sense of meaning and intention as you go through your day.

Help Others: There is nothing more powerful than helping another person. People have often said they were more blessed than the recipient of their help. Helping another person can be big or small—it doesn't matter. Doing good is always good.

Count Your Blessings: Develop an attitude of gratitude. This has been backed by many social science studies. When you consistently review the things for which you are grateful, your mood improves. Try keeping a journal to record what you are grateful for.

It Is Better to Give: "It is better to give than to receive." Giving to another person, cause, organization, or charity gives you a sense of engagement and impact. It broadens your perspectives. You see lives, stories, and needs outside of yourself. Always being self-focused can make you sick. So, instead of buying that thing you don't really need, give money, food, or your time to someone who could use it.

Notice Beauty: Life is full of beautiful things, yet we tend to only notice the negative. Fight that tendency; you may be missing the most enriching aspects of life. Go to an art museum, take a hike, listen to your favorite piece of music, find and tell someone the funniest joke you've ever heard. These may seem like inconsequential things when faced with all the world's problems, but the beautiful side of life is really important. It fills us with a sense of awe and humility. And that has an inestimable value.

Learning to Deal with Stress

> Symptoms surface whenever stress and pressure mount: people become cynical, critical, or silent or they start yelling and overreacting.
>
> Stephen Covey[38]

Stress is one of the most researched of psychological and physical human experiences. Yet, given all that we know, people are still poor managers of their stress. People are slow to recognize stress, resistant to handle it in a healthy way, and then upset that it's ruined sleep, diet, and happiness. So, why are we so bad when it comes to dealing with our stress? Let's take a look at how stress affects your body and brain, and then discuss some solutions.

The Four F's

Researchers have discovered the typical responses people have when exposed to high stress. They were originally called the "Three F's," but the number has grown to the now-current Four F's: *Fight, Flight, Freeze,* and *Feed.* These are in-built survival mechanisms that take over when we are in a dangerous situation.

To illustrate, imagine you are in the jungle, and a tiger jumps out from behind a bush. What do you do?

---

[38] Covey, Stephen R. (2013). *The 7 Habits of Highly Effective People: Powerful Lessons in Personal Change* (25th Anniversary Edition), RosettaBooks, Kindle Locations 2576-2577.

Generally, people would either freeze, take flight, or fight. These are useful responses performed without thinking. The tiger jumps out, and your system is flooded with a stress hormone called cortisol. This stress hormone heightens your physical and mental resources so that whatever you decide in the survival situation, you will have the resources to do so.

Stress has a way of compelling immediate action, which, as in the example given above, has a survival value. However, in non-survival situations, stress reduces our ability to rationally respond to circumstances.

Let's say you are not in a situation of physical danger and something stressful happens. Physiologically, all the same mechanisms activate: brain resources are directed to the primitive/instinctual areas, you'll respond with one of the Four F stress responses, and the learning from your FO kicks in. When all of these factors are kicking-in without your awareness, the results can be disastrous.

The areas of the brain which are responsible for our ability to make judgements, sequentially think through a problem, analyze social cues, and control our impulses is shut down. When stressed, people say and do things they regret, leaving us with questions like "Why did I yell?"; "Why did I immediately get defensive?"; "Why did I perceive my child's question as an attack?" What keeps us alive in life-threatening situations sabotages us at home, at work, and with friends. So, what are some of the emotional/relational consequences of having unchecked stress?

A parent who is stressed often bases their parenting decisions on their level of exhaustion, not on rational thoughts or values. They give in to their child's demands because it would take more energy not to. In fact, discipline becomes such a chore, and exhausted parents will do anything to get their children to stop the bad behavior. This can manifest in multiple ways. For example, your daughter throws a tantrum at the grocery store. She saw some candy and started demanding it. At first, you ignore her, hoping she'll stop. Your daughter sees that you are ignoring her, and instead of stopping, she cries even louder to get your attention. You give her a stern look. She responds with screaming. Other people are now giving *you* that look. What do you do? Stand your ground and draw more attention and embarrassment, or stop your child's whining and give-in? Do you fight fire with fire and yell back at her? Do you avoid the situation and try to get away from the conflict? Maybe you buy a few candy bars for yourself and eat them all?

First of all, your response to this stressor, more than likely, arises out of the ways in which you responded to stressors in your family growing up. Second, the way you respond to stress doesn't make you a bad person. But your stress response comes with costs and benefits. Thankfully, there are ways of decreasing the costs while increasing the benefits. And the way to do this is to understand the triggers that create stress, address family of origin issues, increase something psychologists call *distress tolerance*, and make a plan.

Triggers

Stress doesn't come out of nowhere. It is brought on by a feeling, thought, or event. Therefore, the first step in getting control of your stress is recognition. You need to be able to recognize the things that trigger stress. One way to accomplish this task is to create and maintain a log throughout your week. Be ruthlessly honest and record every time you shut down, explode, avoid, over- or under-eat, or engage in risky sexual behavior. By doing this, you'll be able to recognize patterns. You'll be able to understand the *how*, *when*, *where*, *who*, and *what* of you stress response.

Family of Origin Issues

The family that you grew up in also plays an important formative role. Regardless of how far you may have removed yourself from your family, what you learned growing up with always be with you. Your family environment either shaped you to respond to stress in healthy and positive ways, or it influenced you to respond to stress in negative and unhealthy ways. You'll never be able to grow personally unless you address how your family dealt with stress, conflict, and communication. Examine how your family responded to problems, how they communicated, how they worked through conflict, and problem-solved. Are you acting out what you learned in your family? Where do you need to unlearn what your family taught you and to relearn new ways of living?

Distress Tolerance

Distress tolerance is your capacity to withstand stress. Some have a higher capacity than others—they have *high distress tolerance* (HDT); some have a lower capacity—a *low distress tolerance* (LDT). When faced with stress, a person with HDT doesn't lash out (fight), avoid conflict (flight), shut down (freeze), undertake risky sexual behavior (fornicate), or under- or over-eat (feed). A person with HDT doesn't simply react. They recognize and manage their stress responses so that they can make wise and healthy choices. How do they manage stress? They identify the trigger, choose not to act out what they learned in their FO, and do something to either distract or calm themselves so that they can think clearly. Once they've calmed down, they can problem-solve and bring about a good outcome. These people control their stress instead of being controlled by their stress.

Plan

Having identified what things trigger your stress and what you learned in your family, once you further set yourself up for success by building a high distress tolerance, you already have much to be proud of. But I would make one final suggestion: have a plan. Preparation involves having a strategy to manage stress when you are triggered.

I worked with three clients who exemplified how to effectively use a plan to manage stress. My first client—we'll call him Bob—struggled with alcohol addiction. During counseling, Bob identified what triggered his desire to drink. He also realized that was how his family managed pain: they self-medicated with drugs. We worked on a few ideas to increase his distress tolerance so that he could either distract himself from the desire to drink or soothe his pain through healthy means without resorting to alcohol. Bob was a man of faith, so he decided to pray when he felt triggered to drink. Prayer didn't totally remove the cravings, but it helped. We also made a plan for things Bob could do to help him not drink. The soothing and distraction achieved by prayer allowed Bob to make a choice: he could either act on the plan we had created or he could fall into old habits.

Don't be a victim of stress. Recognize your triggers, understand what you learned growing up in your family, develop distress tolerance, and have a plan. It's incredibly hard work, but your life is being suffocated by stress. Take control back from stress.

reflexive behavior, like isolation, over- or under-sleeping, over- or under-eating, substance abuse, conflict avoidance, poor communication, or emotional neediness. But do these survival behaviors really help us survive? In order to protect ourselves, we really end up hurting ourselves and those around us.

By way of contrast, vulnerability is the opposite of survival mode. Vulnerability is the opposite of denial, avoidance, lashing out, and self-medication. Vulnerability is the strength to face weakness. Through vulnerability, relationships are deepened, self-understanding is gained, and change becomes possible.

Don't let your life be ruled by fear. Don't miss out on the kind of life you know you want but are afraid to take.

Survival Mode Defined

A TV show I really enjoy is *True Detective* on HBO. Season 2 features Detective Ray Velcoro (played by Colin Farrell) and the complicated relationship he has with his son. He loves his son dearly and tries to protect him. At the same time, he's frustrated by his son's lack of traditional masculinity. His son is heavier than the other kids and gets picked on. In the first episode of season 2, he told his son to be "strong." In the second episode, Velcoro arrives at school to find his son missing his shoes. They were taken and destroyed by a bully. While intoxicated, Velcoro forces his son to tell him the name of the bully. He goes to the bully's house and assaults the young man's father, and warns that if the bully ever hurts another person again, he would come back and do even worse damage to his dad.

Although Velcoro did something extreme, assaulting the student's father with brass knuckles, many in our culture, or at least men, would resonate with what he did. Velcoro stood up for his son. He gave the bully some of his own medicine. And he's teaching his son to be "strong." But is this really being "strong?" I would argue that it's not. In fact, I think Velcoro was being weak. "Huh?" you might be saying. "How was he being weak when he just beat someone up? At the very least, he was doing what any father would naturally want to do. How could he be wrong?"

Too many people in our culture identify what is *natural* with what is morally justifiable. In fact, the character Velcoro even mentioned that he had the right to retaliate under "natural law." However, what is natural is not always right. Velcoro did what he did because he went into *survival mode*. Maybe you wouldn't do the same. Perhaps your own survival mode would drive your behavior in other ways, and yet, it might be equally unhealthy.

What is survival mode? Survival Mode is a way of thinking and behaving that is:

- Short-sighted
- Reactive
- Something we regret afterwards
- A pattern of behavior that perpetuates problems
- Hurts ourselves and our relationships

Velcoro models survival mode. His actions were reactive. He was angry and wanted to lash out. After learning about his son's mistreatment, he immediately went to the bully's home and beat his father. And while hurting the bully made him feel better, but it did nothing to fix the problem. His son still didn't know how to stand up for himself. He still couldn't accept his son for who he was.

Your survival mode, whatever it may be, is usually brought on by stress. It is your go-to vice that makes you feel better in the moment and worse in the long run. It is a focus on the symptoms but not the cause. It casts blame on others and refuses personal responsibility. It is the opposite of vulnerability.

Vulnerability Defined

So, what is vulnerability? Let's not kid ourselves: there is a reason no one wants to be vulnerable. It's difficult and uncomfortable. It's difficult to admit to a problem. Vulnerability takes courage, patience, and resilience. These qualities are a must if you are going to break denial and face a problem. In the case of Velcoro, it would have been more difficult to seek a peaceful resolution, to sit down face to face with his son's bully, to see him as a person and not lash out. Yet, when we can commit to a vulnerable course of action, real discussion can happen: honest self-disclosure opens others up.

But such vulnerability is risky. Vulnerability is hard to attain because it's uncomfortable. It's uncomfortable to be honest because honesty doesn't allow us to shape the truth in a way that protects our ego. Velcoro struggled to accept that his son didn't fit and was struggling socially. Velcoro didn't want to recognize that his son may in fact have been struggling because their relationship was faltering. These are hard possibilities to face since we may bear responsibility for the pain our loved ones feel. So, survival mode dictates that we cast blame on someone else. Too often, we run away from the problems that haunt us because, if we were to face them, we might have to change. Yet growth, maintaining healthy relationships, and overcoming problems are only possible if we can take responsibility and work towards change.

Vulnerability—The Bedrock of Relationships

Vulnerability means allowing those we love the most to struggle. This is hard, too—I get that! We are a nation of fixers and problem-solvers. We are more comfortable when taking over, gaining control, and finding solutions than we are with listening, understanding, and supporting. But does this help those around us? Solutions are great, but people aren't problems to be fixed. We actually hurt those around us when we try to fix them or their situation. People don't need to be fixed. They are not machines with broken parts that are easily repaired.

The sad reality is that when trying to solve and fix another person's situation, you may think you are being loving when, in fact, you are not. People need listeners. They need fellow sojourners—others who will walk with them as they struggle. Your friend diagnosed with cancer needs you to sit with her in silence. Your child who doesn't fit in school needs you to simply hold them as they cry. Your mother needs you to hold her hand as she grieves the loss of her partner. Listening while not fixing is a hard thing to do. It is hard to be present with another person, to be empathetic, to play the supportive role and not lead.

Vulnerability demands from us that we enter into another person's struggle and discomfort for the sake of their well-being. Too often, we avoid the pain and struggle of others because it makes us uncomfortable. We don't like to listen; we'd rather take action. We'd rather give advice than try to understand.

Vulnerability seeks to empower those we care about. So, if your friend, child, or family member is struggling, instead of trying to fix them, listen to them. Help them process what is going on. Show them love and compassion. Affirm their voice. Try to understand the situation and how they feel about it. Once you can articulate with empathy what the other is going through, then you can offer suggestions. Do this by empowering. Point out their strengths, highlight the times in the past they overcame obstacles, and help them consider alternatives. And, please, don't put any timelines on them. Don't expect the other person to change in the manner you would like, or when you would like.

I realize what I've said about vulnerability requires a paradigm shift from what we've been taught by our culture, but the shift is so needed. You don't need to revolutionize culture: start simply with a personal revolution. Be the example. Share openly and honestly with those you trust. Face your demons and don't live in denial. Enter into what is uncomfortable and difficult.

Vulnerability may not come to you naturally. That's okay. Learning a new way of living is possible, and vulnerability can be learned. Start with listening courageously, empathizing generously, sharing openly, understanding deeply. Start not by fixing other people but by empowering them. Start by finding strength in your weakness, admitting one problem and asking for help.

Learning the Power of Identity

> Know thyself.
>
> Socrates[40]

The movie *Joy* starring Jennifer Lawrence, Bradley Cooper, and Robert De Niro was a huge hit in 2015. Lawrence plays a struggling single mom surrounded by a family of mooches. The story begins with two sisters being ripped from each other due to their parents' divorce. After that, one tragedy leads to another, but Joy (Lawrence) is the glue that keeps the family together, and she does so at the cost of her own ambitions of being a creator/inventor. Apart from the gripping story, two lessons were demonstrated in the movie: the power of your identity, and the resilience it gives you in the face of adversity.

Fighting from a Position of Weakness

Throughout the film, Joy had to fight many battles. She did this when everything was against her. She had demanding family members, an inflexible job, and a competitor who was trying to steal her design for a self-wrenching mop. Joy was in a disadvantaged position in beginning to fight these battles. But she didn't allow her apparent weakness to paralyze her

---

[40] The aphorism is typically attributed to Socrates, although the maxim predates Socrates and has been attributed to many notable Greek sages such as Thales of Miletus, Pythagoras of Samos among others.

from the fight. This is a key point: people often think they need to have it all together in order to fight the battles that face them. This simply is not true. There will never be a time that is convenient. You will never be able to delay a battle so that you are better positioned to fight it. The only way to be able to fight a battle when one arises is by knowing who you are.

Who Are You?

Sadly, life is inherently unfair. We don't get the breaks we want or deserve. People treat us poorly. Opportunities are missed or taken away. And life rarely seems to bend to our desires. But you must ask yourself this question: is life this way because it's designed for us to fail, or because we give in too quickly when there's a struggle?

Like most things, the answer is probably somewhere in the middle. Yes, there are things that are outside your control that go wrong. Such is life, and there's not much you can do about it. Tires go flat on the highway, family members get sick, the economy changes (sometimes in our favor and sometimes not), and your favorite NFL team loses their seat to the playoffs year after year. "Qué será, será," right? But this axiom of reality does not extend to everything. There are other things in your life that are attainable, that can be changed or controlled. Attaining them, however, may come with a battle.

The things that are within your control—that can be attained but may not be easy—are within your grasp as long as you know who you are. So, let me ask you, who are you?

Socrates, the Athenian philosopher of ancient Greece, thought this was the most important question you could ask yourself. He also thought of himself as a gadfly because he would irritate or disrupt people's lives by forcing them, through questions, to look at unexamined areas of their lives. Plato recorded Socrates' famous saying "The unexamined life is not worth living!" Through the process of examination, the targets of Socrates questions' were "born" into the truth. In other words, Socrates was helping give birth, like a midwife, to the truth of who his conversants were. This idea if self-knowledge is not just an interesting ancient artifact. The power of Socrates' philosophy still impacts people today. Knowing who you are, your identity, can provide you with the knowledge to change, the power to act, the confidence to stand your ground, and the possibility of self-acceptance.

To discover who you are, start by asking yourself some basic questions: "What are my values? Who do I look up to? What do I think is right and wrong? What kind of behavior do I tolerate from other people? What is important to me? What are my goals in life? What do I want my legacy to be?

Why are these questions important? When life throws you a situational curve ball or puts a difficult person in your path, you are challenged at your core. Your beliefs, your self-concept, your values and preferences will come under attack. If you don't know who you are, you are liable to change for the situation or the person in ways that don't benefit you or don't reflect who you are.

You may have heard the old adage "A man who stands for nothing will fall for anything."[41] If the foundation of your life isn't firmly established, someone or something can come along and knock you down. Let's say, for example, that your boss at work wants you to do something unethical to advance the interests of the company. What do you do? Allow your boss to have his way at the cost of your own ethics? At the risk of being caught and taking the blame? This could have serious implications. You could lose your job, be blacklisted from your industry, and develop a bad reputation. So, what do you do? This isn't a theoretical question or one for the philosophers; this is a question, a dilemma, a matter of identity that happens every day. *Who you are determines what you do.* If you are a person of principle, of sound ethics, this would violate what you believe and threaten your integrity—and what you should do would be clear. If you were unsure, then you could be persuaded to do something wrong and personally harmful. What you do is determined by who you are.

When someone blocks you from attaining your goals because of their selfishness, you know that they need to be challenged. Too often, we allow others to get away with murder because we have no clue of who we are. This is where we meet up with Joy again.

Don't Buy the Story Sold to You

Joy hit rock bottom. Her product was selling, but due to material costs being hiked up, a sister who made a bad

---

[41] Gordon A. Eadie (1945) *The Over-All Mental-Health Needs of the Industrial Plant, with Special Reference to War Veterans*. Mental Hygiene, Vol 1, Num 29.

deal with her production company, and the inevitable failure of a lawsuit, Joy gave up and signed a bankruptcy declaration. But all the failures didn't make her throw in the towel. So, what pushed her over the edge to admit defeat? It was her father blaming himself for "allowing" his daughter to "Think she was more than a broke housewife." He went on to say he had given her too much confidence that she believed she could achieve more than she could. It was her father's words that put the final nail in the coffin. She bought the story her father had sold her. Fortunately, that's not where the story ends.

After she signed the declaration and everyone went their separate ways, something about what her father said bothered her. She didn't think he was right. She returned the story he had sold her. The "line" her family was forcing on her didn't fit with her identity. She wasn't a quitter; she wasn't a broke housewife suffering from over-confidence. She spent that night pouring over her patent, contract agreements, and other legal paperwork to see if she was getting a raw deal. The next scene cuts to her in Texas as she meets with the owner of her production company. She coolly points out all the ways she's cheated and how her lawyers are chomping at the bit for a lawsuit, but she decided to see if this owner would have a change of heart. He looks at her and starts naming off what he's willing to give her in exchange for no lawsuit. She is silent while he squirms. He ends up compensating her for all the money she's rightfully owed with interest!

The story now cuts away to Joy triumphantly walking down the street with a big smile on her face as a loud rock and roll anthem blares out. The triumphant rock music with the slow walk-away is where Hollywood takes over and real life ends, but there is an element of truth in Joy's story, especially since the movie is based on a real person and real events. Joy was able to do what she did because she knew who she was. She knew the story her dad sold her wasn't true—she didn't buy it any more. She knew something unjust had been done to her, and that that injustice threatened the loss of her dream. There really was only one course of action: fight.

You will have struggles and battles in your life. That much goes without saying. But the question that will determine if you fight, if you find your voice and use it, if you stand up for your dream is: *Do you know who you are?*

Learning to Grieve and Adapt

The only thing that is constant is change.
                                    Heraclitus

Growth in the business world can be paradoxical. On the one hand, companies have to keep changing to different consumer trends, adapting to the marketplace, and challenging themselves to better. But what if a company does all those things and is successful? That's a good thing, right? Well, yes and no. Success is a good thing, but it comes with a hidden danger.

Success has a way of becoming the status quo. Makes sense, "If it ain't broke, don't fix it." But here's the danger; the status quo can be the enemy of change. That is to say, what worked to get initial success won't work in the long run. "What got us here won't get us there" is a rather well-known axiom in the business world that speaks to the need for change and adaptation.

Some companies hit it big. Out of all the hundreds of companies that fail, there are the special few that succeed. But success isn't enough to create longevity: the reason being that success makes companies comfortable. They go into cruise control. A contemporary example of this is McDonald's. In the 90s, McDonald's was the "it" company. Their commercials were popular, their company mascot was beloved by the nation's children, and their brand was more recognizable than the names of Albert Einstein or

George Washington. McDonald's was a moneymaking machine, to say the least. At the height of their success, McDonald's had 30,000 locations spanning 100 countries. They were (and still are) a multinational, multibillion-dollar company. So, would you be surprised to hear they are declining? In the last few years McDonald's has been in a financial freefall. They desperately attempted to salvage their profits by adding espresso to their menu, making more menu items "gourmet," and, most recently, making the breakfast menu available all day long. But these efforts have only slowed revenue bleeding. So, how did the most popular company of the 90s nosedive in the last decade?

McDonald's kept growing—in size—but they stopped growing in terms of innovation and market demand. In other words, they stopped adapting to what people wanted. American culture has changed. People today don't want a fatty, salty, sugary meal made from sources that have questionable production methods. What got them big wins in the 90s hasn't sustained them through the 2010s.

The logic that guides the business world also applies to the world of mental health. What could save McDonald's could save you.

Change and Loss

Change is inevitable. We can't avoid change as much as we may like to. Kids grow older, the job market shifts, relationships drift apart, physical health breaks down. What worked for you yesterday may not yield the same successes today. So, what can you do to keep adapting?

The first step is to face the fact that change means loss. Think about it. When a friend moves across the country, part of you is missing. Or, let's say, you lose your job: a major part of your identity is now missing. Maybe you're going through a divorce, or someone close to you is. That relationship—that love once shared—that story has ended. Every change is like the death of what was. You can either acknowledge that death, which gives birth to the new, or you can ignore it and stay dead.

Also, change to your life isn't always simply *like* death: sometimes you have to deal with death itself. I've worked with many clients who are dealing with the loss of a parent, child, spouse, sibling, or friend. For them, grieving is necessary to accept the loss. It allows them to adapt to their new life. Yet grieving is a choice, a choice to reorient and restructure your life after the change or loss. Grieving is important because the life you once had is gone. I've seen far too many people pining for a life they no longer have. They are effectively living in the past. So, what's the lesson that must be learned? How do you move forward after change? How do you adapt?

Healthy Grief

An indispensable element of adaptation is the healthy habit of grieving. "But isn't grief sad, something that I should avoid?" By no means! Grief is not only an indisputable reality of life, but it is also good and healthy. There is such a thing as "good grief," as Charlie Brown would say. But, sadly, far too many people have no concept of what healthy grief looks like. People often think that grief is just feeling sad for a while—and that, eventually, you're not so sad anymore.

This couldn't be further from the truth. There are actually four tasks involved in healthy grief.[42]

Task 1—Accept the Reality of the Loss: You must confront your own denial that part of your life is gone. Your life has changed, and that's okay. You can't move forward until you face reality.

Task 2—Experience the Pain of Grief: For whatever reason, we are afraid to feel in our culture. We take pills, distract ourselves with entertainment and generally avoid discomfort, but this isn't helping us. This is compounding our pain. Instead, experience the pain of what you have lost. It is the only way for you to accept the reality of what happened.

Task 3—Adjust to an Environment with the Deceased Missing: Life is not the same now that your marriage has ended, your friend has moved away, your job is gone or your child has died. You must find a new normal. Don't try to recreate what you had. Take what's in front of you and work with that.

Task 4—Find an Enduring Connection with the Deceased While Embarking on a New Life: Even though that part of you is gone and irretrievable as a result of the change, it is still part of who you are. Memories are the foundation of your identity. Cherish what you have lost while moving forward.

---

[42] Worden, J. William, *Grief Counseling and Grief Therapy: A Handbook for the Mental Health Practitioner*, Springer Publishing Company, p. 84.

Notice that these tasks aren't "stages," which would otherwise imply that grief is something you are carried through passively. Each task requires effort, work, and engagement. You must be the driver in your own grieving process. Engaging in the hard work of these four tasks allows you to move forward.

I once worked with a woman who lost her mother. The death was sudden— without warning. My client stated to me that she was shocked when it happened and the feeling of disbelief stuck with her for years following. She could not come to grips with the reality of her mom's loss. Therefore, the pain she felt every time she thought about her mom caused tremendous pain, even several years later.

When we started counseling, accepting the reality of the loss was our first step. We did this by discussing who the client's mom was, what she meant to her, and what is different now that she's gone. Although painful to discuss, going through these questions made her mom's death more concrete. She was able to process her feelings, something she wasn't able to do since the feelings were so powerful and overwhelming. The more she talked, the less overwhelmed she felt. She was finally letting herself feel. She was overcoming her denial.

She came to an understanding by denying her mother's death, she didn't have to deal with it. But this kept her stuck. She wasn't living, she was just "existing." Her mom's death was such a key moment in her life, it was clouding everything else she had going on. She had two incredible sons, a caring husband and an interesting career. But those things were appreciated by the client because her mind was preoccupied with her mom. Coming to grips with her mom's death allowed her to enjoyed what she had.

After time, my client could think of her mom without pain. This was very helpful because there were so many good memories my client had of her mom. Her mom was wise, kind and empathetic. Her advice was still relevant to the client. Her voice still empowering and her legacy still inspiring even though she was gone. This was the enduring connection my client was looking for.

Moving Forward

Accepting the fact that life is constantly changing—and that with those changes comes loss, or that with loss comes change—allows you to process grief in a healthy way. And, as I said above, healthy grief empowers you to move forward, which is a key piece in adapting. Then, and only then, can you adjust to a new normal and continue with the stuff of life. But too many want the "moving forward" part without the hard work. That kind of "cheap moving forward" isn't really moving forward at all. It's more ignoring and avoiding, which actually accomplishes the opposite of moving forward. It instead keeps you stuck.

Cheap moving forward cements you where you are. Everything around you (places, people, and things) may change, but, inside, you are still in that same place. True moving forward isn't cheap. It will cost you something. You will have to face painful things. You'll have to accept what is no more. You will have to engage in the four tasks of grief. But the payoff is the ability to move forward. So, you have to ask yourself, "Is the cost of moving forward worth it?" Healthy grieving enriches you as a person. It's not easy, that's for sure, but what in life is? The things that people cherish the most are typically things that bear the greatest cost. Ask yourself, "Is the cost of healthy grieving so scary that I'm willing to lose out on the benefit of moving forward?"

Learning to Control What You Can, Not What You Can't

> God, grant me the serenity
> to accept the things I cannot change,
> the courage to change the things I can,
> and the wisdom to know the difference.
> Reinhold Niebuhr[43]

Maybe you've heard the expression "You can't change another person; you can only change yourself." Do you think this is true? Many of us would agree, but not many of us actually live in a way that is consistent with the statement. Just admit it. You've tried to change someone you were in a relationship with before. To be honest, it's hard not to. There are people in our lives that we love, but they rub us the wrong way. If only one or two things were different about them, they'd be perfect. This notion seems innocent enough, but if acted on, the wreckage caused to relationships is incalculable.

If you are or have been guilty of trying to change another person, I have three questions: First, what kind of damage has trying to change another person caused? Second, why do you do it? And third, how to change this bad habit?

Trying to Change Another Person

---

[43] Niebuhr, Reinhold (1987). *The Essential Reinhold Niebuhr: Selected Essays and Addresses*, edited by Robert McAfee Brown, Yale University Press; New Ed edition, p. 251.

If you are trying to forcibly change your husband or wife, partner, child, friend, parent, co-worker or family members, don't. Stop immediately because it's not working. Worse than that, it's making you miserable and hurting the other person. Why do I say this? I've seen too many of my clients try it. I can tell you unhesitatingly, it doesn't do any good. People aren't broken machines that can be fixed by replacing a part. People don't work that way. People in intimate relationships don't respond to force. Instead, people respond to the influence and suggestions of others who they know, beyond a shadow of a doubt, has their best interest at heart.

Why People Try to Change Other People

But, if attempts to control others cause so much damage, why do people do it? Other people do this of selfishness, pure and simple. We think we know how someone else ought to live their lives. They would be so much better if they were *this way* versus *that way*. But we're really not trying to change them for their benefit, are we? No, we are trying to mold them into something for our benefit. We are imposing our preferences on them. This always causes hurt and damage.

Believing that you know the right way for how another person should be is a rather arrogant mindset and not terribly respectful to the other person. Take a moment and imagine that someone was forcibly trying to change you. I'm guessing you wouldn't be very open to what they're trying to say. Or what if that person assumed they were right about a decision and forced you to see it their way? Whether they're right or wrong, their approach is disrespectful and off-putting, right? *In communication, approach matters as much as the importance of the message.* You can win the battle but lose the war when you approach important conversations from a position of superiority.

The old adage rings true: "People don't care how much you know until they know how much you care."[44] Even if you have great insight, some good feedback, or a great point, the person sitting across from you needs to know that you care about them before they are able to receive what you have to say. That means you must lead with respect. Show them the respect you would like to receive yourself, then offer up what you have to say.

What Can You Do to Change?

If you struggle with control, what can you do to change? The very best thing you can do is realize that you cannot change another person. If you try, it will lead you down a path of disrespect and meanness—and, from there, regret. *People respond to respect.*

So, other than with people, what about the ways we deal with general life conditions? The same thinking applies. You can't control situations, either. When it comes to the economy, who gets elected, downsizing in your company, interest rates, or fertility, these are simply out of your direct control. If you struggle with anxiety, ask yourself if you are trying to control things

---

[44] Theodore Roosevelt as quoted in John Maxwell's book *Winning with People: Discover the People Principles that Work for You Every Time*, p. 91.

outside your reach. This speaks to an idea that is important for mental health: how you view control in your life.

You need to understand what is within your control, your *internal locus of control*—and what is outside your control, your *external locus of control*. Those things within your control you can work to change. Those things outside your control you must radically accept. Let's take a closer look at these two categories.

Different Views of Control

Your loci of control can be "internal" or "external": these are helpful terms for identifying where you psychologically locate control in your life. "Internal" refers to what is within you; "external" is whatever is outside of you.

Internal Locus of Control

What is in your control are things that you can directly influence or change. For example, you can directly control what you eat, when you go to bed, how much water you drink in a day, how you respond to co-workers, and how often you look at your smartphone. No one else can make you do these things; they are totally and completely done at your choosing. While you can't control the weather or shifts in the economy, you can control how you respond to those things. You can't change your spouse, but you can change how you respond to your spouse. Get the idea?

External Locus of Control

The things you would put in the external category are what you cannot or should not try to control. Like I said above, you can't control the shifts in the economy, the behavior of your co-workers, the attitudes of your spouse, or the weather. These things operate independently of you. Many people try to control what they cannot. This can make them unhappy, mentally ill, or a "control freak."

Help! I'm a Controller

In order to get help, you must first admit you have tried to control others. Then you must admit that the control approach simply doesn't work and causes relational damage. Take the next step and sort out what your view of control is. Accept what is outside your control. And redirect your energy and attention to change what within your control.

You can only influence other people, you cannot control them. Influence is achieved by your approach AND by how you respond to your boss, co-worker, child, spouse, partner or friend. *Approach* and *response* are very different *control* and *force*. If your approach is respectful, generally, people will be open to your influence and persuasion, especially when it comes from someone whom they trust. If you really want to "change" your spouse, child, friend, or co-worker, then earn their trust, have their best in mind, and try to influence them through respectful suggestions and reason. That approach will preserve the relationship and get you the best results.

Hopefully, distinguishing between internal and external locus of control will help you. *The more you try to control what you can't, the more miserable you will be.* So, determine what and who are truly outside of your control, and accept that reality. This is hard to do, so take a deep breath and say along with me,

"God, grant me the serenity
to accept the things I cannot change,
the courage to change the things I can,
and the wisdom to know the difference."

Learning How to Identify What Hurts Your Sex Life

> Good sex begins while your clothes are still on.
> Masters and Johnson[45]

The sexual relationship shared between intimate partners has been compared to a dance. The analogy is quite fitting. In dancing, there are both missteps and moments of brilliance, ecstasy, partnership, teamwork, trust, and practice. If the dancers don't trust each other, they'll always be holding back. If there's no teamwork, their steps will be out of sync. And if they never practice, performance will always be lacking. The same goes for physical intimacy.

Sex is an indicator of the quality of the relationship. If partners don't communicate well, that effects their sex life. If partners don't trust each other, their sex life will become non-existent. Therefore, it is critical to identify the proverbial missteps so that you can pick up on the hints of deeper problems. If you don't, given enough missteps, the dancers will give up and go home. In other words, the relationship will slowly fade away. This doesn't have to be you and your relationship. Inside each misstep is a lesson. So, let's learn the dance of a healthy sex life.

---

[45] Bill Masters and Virginia Johnson quoted in Paulman, Paul; Taylor, Robert; Paulman, Audry; Nasir, Laeth (2016). *Family Medicine: Principles and Practice*, Springer, p. 504.

Knowing the Difference

Men and women are different. Well, no duh! Generally, men are visually turned on, and they think about sex far more than women—and for men, sex is primarily a physical act of pleasure. On the other hand, women, in general, don't think about sex with the same frequency as men. Furthermore, women are turned on by relational connection and foreplay, and enjoy the bond and connection enhanced by sex. These differences are important. Knowing the differences between men and women is key because partners often initiate, seduce, and make love in the way that makes sense to them. Typically, men want sex fast and furious, whereas women prefer sex to be warm and intimate. So, when initiating sex with your partner, consider their needs and preferences. If your sex life centers on your preferences and needs only, you run the risk of hurting your sex life.

Rejection

It is like salt on a wound when a partner's sexual advance is rejected. It's unrealistic to expect that every single advance will be well received, but if you're consistently shot down or shooting down the other person, that kills desire. Being rejected hurts. It's awkward and kind of embarrassing.

If you are the one shooting down the other, tell them why you are shooting them down. You need to communicate what you want. If you are the one being shot down, ask why you are being shot down. Maybe there's something wrong in your approach. Maybe your partner doesn't feel cared for or understood. Don't let rejection shut you down. You need to communicate and try to understand why you are being rejected.

Treating Sex like a Chore

I get it. You've had a long day and you have a lot on your mind. But please don't treat sex like it's another thing to check off your to-do list. Sex is fun, exciting, bond-forming, playful, and passionate. When you treat sex like a chore, your partner can tell. They can sense when you are going through the motions and don't really care. That hurts. That kills the fun and the passion. Instead, try to make it fun, new, and interesting. This doesn't mean you have to spend a lot of money or do outrageous things. Try simple things like giving your partner a long backrub before sex. Buy them a treat on your way home from work. Leave them an unexpected note. These small steps break up the monotony and add thoughtfulness and affection into the mix.

Being Self-Conscious

When you are feeling overly self-conscious, it hurts the sexual experience. Your partner can tell when you're more worried about how you look than about connecting with them. Sex for your partner is not about performance. It's about forgetting the worries of the day, being passionate, and connecting with and enjoying one another. But when you make it about how you look or how you are performing, this diminishes the experience.

Next time you starting feeling self-conscious before or during sex, change your perspective. Remind yourself that your partner loves you, that they are sexually attracted to you— why else would they be having sex with you? And most importantly, feel confident. Confidence is tremendously sexy. Take ownership for your body and accept yourself.

Staying in Your Comfort Zone

Sex is a bodily, fleshy, earthy kind of thing. There are fluids, sweat, and noises. But what did you expect? You are using your body to connect with another human being. It's a bodily experience. Embrace the messiness of sex. It doesn't have to be perfect and tidy. Enjoy it for what it is. But, if you want to manage sex and keep it in your comfort zone, that will hurt the experience.

I challenge you to take a risk. Surprise your partner by engaging in one of their fantasies. Or, act out one of your fantasies. Have sex in a new position or location. Have sex at a different time of day than you normally have it. Come home for lunch just to have sex. Change it up and get outside your comfort zone.

Consider Your Partner's Needs

If sex, for you, is all about your needs, expect your partner to feel left out. Your partner likes making you feel good. In fact, they feel good when they can make you feel good. But, if it's always going one way, sex can be unsatisfying. Sex is about mutual satisfaction. It is an act of giving and receiving. If all you do is take, it can build resentment in the other. Change it up sometimes. Ask your partner what they would like.

Or if, on the other hand, your partner is the one who is being selfishness, beware! If you don't tell your partner how you feel, you will begin to resent them. It's better to talk with them about your feelings and work on a solution.

Being Routine

If all you ever do is the "same ol' same ol'," expect sex to get boring. Routine is the enemy of passion. It's okay to be spontaneous every once in a while. Surprise your partner with something new in the bedroom, or, like I said before, have sex at an unexpected time. Also, it's not just about when you have sex, but how you have sex. Don't become routine with positions or foreplay. Get a book, buy some new music, read a blog, and mix it up. Try new things. It may be hit or miss, but whether it works or not, it shows that you care.

Making it Conditional

If you make sex conditional upon your partner fulfilling some agenda of yous, that is a major misstep. Let's say you have a disagreement and refuse sex because your partner doesn't agree with you. That's a bad precedent to set. You are using sex as a bargaining chip, and that's not what sex is for. It is a shared privilege between the two of you. It is not something for you to give or take away based upon *getting what you want*. You must consider the needs of the other. Sex is a vital aspect of any romantic partnership, but once it becomes conditional, it is no longer a shared element of your relationship.

Mind-Reading

If you your partner to always know when you are in the mood, without giving any signals, you are setting your partner up for failure. You can't expect your partner to be a mind-reader. You need to communicate your needs. But there is a caveat to this: intimate partners should be attuned to each other's needs, wants and desires, but it is unreasonable to expect that all the time. Throughout the day, you're juggling several different things: work, family, friends, a social life, kids, bills, responding to emails, and on and on and on. Help your partner out. Communicate that you want to be close to them, that you'd like them to massage your feet, give you a hug, and make love to you. You've got a lot on your mind, and so do they. So, help each other out and don't assume they're ignoring you. Whenever you expect them to mind-read, you're setting your partner and yourself up for frustration.

Control

This section could easily be labeled "Making it Conditional: Part II." If you view sex as a means of gaining control in your relationship, then you're making a huge misstep. Just as you want a sense of shared control over your bank accounts, budget, bills, where you go on your vacation, and whose family you spend time with over the holidays, you also want a shared sense of control over sex. If you are the only one holding the reigns, your partner will resent you. No one likes feeling as if they have no control regarding something as important as sex. Work towards a shared sense of ownership and responsibility regarding your sex life. Teamwork makes the dream work!

Conclusion

There are more things to mention, but hopefully this will stimulate your thinking. If you think you are blameless and your partner is the problem, you're way off. Don't make the mistake of placing all the blame on your partner for the missteps in your sex life. It takes two to tango! Sex is a relational act. Therefore, if there's a problem, it will take both of you to fix it. Be prepared to take responsibility for your missteps. Let your missteps be your teacher. Learn what they are indicating so that you don't keep making the same mistake.

Epilogue

All good things must come to an end.
Geoffrey Chaucer

You have come to the end of this book but not to the end of your journey. Your struggles may seem overwhelming, but rest assured, there is light at the end of the tunnel. Things will get better. You can overcome.

Hopefully, you've learned a few lessons as you've read this book. The worst thing you can do is to feel overwhelmed by all the information. Learning is a process of gaining awareness through trial and error, reflection, and growth. Rome wasn't built in a day, and neither is your life. So, do yourself a favor and take the pressure off.

Be patient with yourself. Personal development is hard. Surround yourself with a community of supportive friends and family members who will learn with you. If you have that, then be the support for another person. If you benefitted from this book, if it helped you take the first step, then help another do the same. Be the friend you needed. Share this book, or at least the insights you gained, with them. Helping another person is the best medicine you can give to yourself.

About the Author

Daniel Bates is a Licensed Mental Health Counselor who works with families dealing with violence, substance abuse, and legal issues. He loves to write, think critically, and drink coffee. He's passionate about writing and reading poetry, discussing philosophy/theology, spending time with his wife and daughters, connecting with friends, and getting lost in a good book. He's fascinated by the intersection of faith/spirituality and mental health. He's written three books of poetry, a nonfiction book on the Christian mystics, and a self-help book on how to use the lessons life teaches us, all of which are available on Amazon in Kindle and paperback formats. Daniel also writes for two online magazines: mum.info and FamilyShare.com, in addition to his own blog. You can find links to Daniel's books, read his blog, and view and purchase his paintings at his website, danielbates.co.

More from Daniel Bates
The Modern Mystic

Wish your spiritual life wasn't mediocre? Is your prayer life dead? Are you jealous of the spiritual vitality that everyone else seems to have except for you? Don't let your life be ruled by a spiritual malaise. Instead of checking out, go further and deeper in to the heart of God.

But how?

The Christian mystics are ancient voices with a modern message. They teach that the love of God is deeper, wider and beyond anything you can understand. It is altogether mysterious and right in front of you. It is the paradoxical truth wrapped in the unimaginable love of a relational God eager to know and be known by you.

Yes, you are the object of God's love. And yes, God is the ultimate source of your happiness. Knowing and experiencing God's love will change you. Yet experiencing God's love is not a destination. It is a journey. And you are a sojourner in need of a guide. Allow the Christian mystics to direct you along the sometimes confusing wandering path of God's love.

When Parenting Backfires

Let's be honest. Parenting is hard. From the moment children take their first breaths, parents are faced with decisions and choices that no manual could ever fully explain. And the way you parent is constantly changing: babies need protection, toddlers need direction, and teens need influence. We as parents are simply expected to do it and do it well.

From two therapists who have a combined 25 years of experience working with families comes a new kind of parenting book. This book doesn't focus on technique, a discipline scheme or parenting style. This book focuses on the parent themselves, specifically the kind of thinking that makes parents effective or ineffective. In *When Parenting Backfires* examines 12 thinking errors commonly made by parents. In each chapter Dan and David:

- Explain the thinking error

- How it backfires
- What parents can do to correct the thinking error
- And real life examples of parents who have recognized their thinking error, made the correction, and improved their effectiveness.

Let this book do its work. Let down your guard and be open to the new ideas. As I've already said, the biggest risk you'll take is to your ego as you improve your parenting skills and your relationship with your kids. I think any effective parent is willing to take those odds. Are you?

Even a Superhero Needs Counseling

Even A Superhero Needs Counseling is an in-depth guide to understanding your favorite comic book character from a psychological perspective while providing you with relevant and insightful advice. In other words, by learning more about Thor, the Hulk, Wonder Woman, Stephen Strange, Superman and many more, you can learn more about yourself. Comic books aren't just entertainment; they can be a window into the strengths and weaknesses of humanity.

Daniel Bates is a Licensed Mental Health Counselor who offers his expert counsel for superhero, supervillain and readers alike. In each chapter, you'll find:

- An overview of major comic book character's origin story, arch-enemies, and dynamics of their psychology.

- A mental health diagnosis based on the relevant details of the character's symptoms.
- What mental health treatment would consist of based on the diagnosis and how it would help their life.
- And, most importantly, how your favorite comic book character's story can be informative for you own personal growth.

So, if you struggle with anxiety you're in good company, Superman can relate. If you've had an addiction, you and Tony Stark could go to an Alcoholics Anonymous meeting together. Or, if you've ever had relationship problems, the Scarlet Witch can commiserate with you. Whatever the problem, you will find a superhero or supervillain that shares your struggle. And it is through their stories, you can find help for yours.

Check Out Daniel's Podcast

Counselor Dan Podcast is a podcast for those who want to be entertained and informed. Counselor Dan Podcast goes deep into the latest research from psychology, the insights from counseling, and the personal experiences Daniel has accrued over his career. You can find the podcast at counselordanpodcast.com. It's also available on Podbean and iTunes.

Check Out Daniel's Website

Daniel's blog, videos, books, and information about counseling services can be found on his website, counselordan.com. the website is a fantastic resource for anyone interested in psychology and mental health. New blogs, podcasts and videos are added to the site every week.

Counseling Services

If you are interested contacting Daniel for counseling, he recently expanded his private practice at Lacamas Counseling in Camas, Washington. You can find information about Daniel's counseling specialties, location of the office or other counselors that may be a fit for you at lacamascounseling.com. He's currently accepting new clients. Email or Call to schedule an appointment.

www.ingramcontent.com/pod-product-compliance
Lightning Source LLC
LaVergne TN
LVHW051600070426
835507LV00021B/2685